WRESTLING

By REX PEERY Coach, University of Pittsburgh

and ARNOLD "SWEDE" UMBACH
Coach, Auburn University, Alabama

STERLING PUBLISHING CO., INC. NEW YORK

Oak Tree Press Co., Ltd.
London & Sydney

ATHLETIC INSTITUTE SERIES

Baseball
Basketball
Girls' Basketball
Girls' Gymnastics

Gymnastics
Judo
Table Tennis
Tumbling and Trampolining
Wrestling

Thirteenth Printing, 1977
Copyright © 1967, 1961
by The Athletic Institute
Published by Sterling Publishing Co., Inc.
Two Park Avenue, New York, N.Y. 10016

Distributed in Australia and New Zealand by Oak Tree Press Co., Ltd.,
P.O. Box J34, Brickfield Hill, Sydney 2000, N.S.W.
Distributed in the United Kingdom and elsewhere in the British Commonwealth
by Ward Lock Ltd., 116 Baker Street, London W 1
Manufactured in the United States of America
Library of Congress Catalog Card No.: 61-12052
Sterling ISBN 0–8069–4334–3 Trade   Oak Tree 7061–2245 3
4335–1 Library

Table of Contents

GLOSSARY OF TERMS*

Arm Bar: A hold secured by encircling the opponent's arm near the armpit with the holder's corresponding arm and placing the palm of the hand against his chest or thigh.

Arm Drag: A maneuver executed by grasping the opponent's upper arm and attempting to pull him to the mat.

Back Heel: Tripping an opponent from behind by placing the foot behind the heel and forcing him over backwards.

Bar Arm: A lock secured by encircling the opponent's upper arm with the crook of the elbow; hands are joined behind the opponent's back. If both arms are encircled and joined behind the opponent's back, it would then be a double bar arm.

Bar Hammerlock: A hold secured against a prone opponent. The opponent's arm is crooked at right angles behind his back, and the attacker slides his arm under the opponent's forearm and grips with his hand on the opponent's upper arm, the attacker's forearm thus being woven through the V of his opponent's upper and lower arm.

Bar Lock: A lock which bars the opponent's arm from effective use.

Body Lock: A lock around the opponent's body with the arms.

Body Press: The exertion of body weight against a supine opponent on the mat in an effort to force both shoulders to the mat and thus secure a fall.

Breakdown: The flattening of the underneath opponent to his stomach or side by removing his hand and knee support.

Bull Neck: The stiffening of the neck; neck is shortened and tucked in while the shoulders are elevated with strain.

Catch-as-Catch-Can: The usual wrestling style in the United States. The wrestler is permitted to hold his opponent below the waist and to trip and tackle. He may also use that part of his body below the waist to secure scissors hold, grapevine and combination arm and leg holds.

Collar and Elbow: A tie-up position whereby the aggressor grasps his opponent's left elbow with his right hand and places his left hand on the neck of his opponent.

---

*Terms were taken from "The Dictionary of Sports," edited and prepared by Parke Cummings and published by A. S. Barnes & Co.,1949.

Crab Ride: A safe riding position. Attacker sits in back of a sitting opponent and locks his arms around the opponent's waist. The attacker holds his legs under the opponent's body with his insteps hooked in back of the opponent's knees.

Cross-Body Ride: A grapevine or scissors hold on the opponent's far or near leg, and locking the opposite arm.

Cross Face: A hold secured by extending the forearm across the side of the opponent's face, and grasping the opponent's far upper arm above the elbow.

Crotch Hold: A hold around the opponent's leg near the crotch or in the center of the crotch.

Double: A hold secured by both the attacker's arms, such as a double wristlock; or a hold secured on two appendages, such as a double arm lock or double leg lock.

Drag: A maneuver executed by grasping the opponent's upper arm and attempting to pull him to the mat.

Drill: To drive the opponent to the mat with force.

Elbow Lock: A lock secured by hooking the opponent's elbow in the crook of the arm; a lock executed prior to rolling the opponent over.

Elevator: A maneuver employed to open up space between bodies in which to effect an escape. This is executed by the wrestler who is underneath on the mat. He uses his legs and arms to lift the opponent and turn him over to the bottom position.

Escape: A maneuver by which a defensive wrestler eludes his opponent. In amateur wrestling each escape scores one point.

Fall: The major objective of the contest resulting when any part of the wrestler's shoulders are held in contact with the mat for an "appreciable" time; in amateur rules, two seconds of silent count.

Fall-Back: A maneuver in which the wrestler stands behind his opponent and then accomplishes a takedown by falling back, thus dragging the opponent to the mat.

Figure-Four Scissors: A hold secured against a prone opponent whereby one leg is thrust all the way under the opponent's body and the foot of this leg is hooked behind the knee of the holder's opposite leg. This foot is then hooked behind the calf of the defender's leg.

Full Nelson: Illegal in amateur wrestling. A hold taken by a wrestler who is behind his opponent. He places both arms under the opponent's arms and clasps his hands or wrists on the back of his opponent's neck.

Grapevine: A weaving hold in which one leg entwines the opponent's leg.

Guillotine: A fall secured from a cross-body ride and a reverse half-nelson.

Half-Nelson: A hold secured when one arm is placed under the opponent's corresponding arm and around the opponent's neck.

Hammerlock: A hold which places the opponent's arm in a right-angle position behind his back. It is legal in amateur wrestling if the arm is not bent above a right angle; i.e., not above the small of the opponent's back.

Headlock: A hold secured by encircling the opponent's head with the arm or arms.

Helmet: A lightweight cloth hood with metal cups or rubber ear pads used in practice; prevents "cauliflower ears."

High Bridge: A position in which the head is turned back so that the face and hands are on the mat with fingers pointed inward. The balls of the feet also support the body and the buttocks are raised more than a foot from the mat.

Hip Lock: A hold usually following the obtaining of a headlock from a standing position. The aggressor turns his back to the opponent's body and forces the opponent's body across his own lower back.

Hook: To reach under or around the opponent's arm or leg, and secure a hold with the hand or crook of the arm.

Key Lock: An arm lock against the opponent's bent arm; is usually secured after successfully completing a double wristlock.

Leg Snap: Tackling of the opponent. The opponent's leg (or legs) is encircled and he is pulled to the mat. Also called leg dive, leg grab and leg pick-up.

Loose Rider: A wrestler who permits his opponent to move around a good deal in the defensive position, but keeps him under control by keeping him off balance.

Pin: To secure a fall; so-called because both of the opponent's shoulder blades are forced or "pinned" to the mat.

Pinning Combination: A combination of holds which results in a fall.

Quarter-Nelson: A hold taken when the holder is kneeling beside a prone opponent. The objective is to lift the opponent's body and turn it over onto the back.

Re-Drag: A counter to a drag.

Referee's Position on the Mat: A position in which the defensive wrestler has both knees on the mat, lower legs parallel, knees not more than shoulder- or hip-width apart and with heels of both hands on the mat not less than 12 inches in front of the knees. The offensive contestant is close to the opponent at either side with his nearest arm loosely around the opponent's waist and other arm at the opponent's elbows. Both knees must be on the mat and opposite the opponent's nearest leg. His rear leg may not touch the near leg of the defensive wrestler.

Reverse Body Lock: A hold against a prone opponent—the wrestler's feet pointing in approximately opposite directions. The attacker's arm is under the opponent's waist and the hand grasping the opponent's side.

Ride: To hold the position of advantage in spite of the opponent's efforts to escape.

Scissors Hold: A hold secured by locking the legs at the instep or ankles around any part of the opponent's body. The holder applies pressure with the inner parts of his knees, his legs stretching.

Sit-Out: A maneuver when a wrestler is underneath (kneeling) in "referee's position on the mat." He comes to a sitting position as a preliminary move to follow-up maneuvers in an effort to escape or to gain a reverse position.

Slam: Illegal in amateur wrestling. Lifting the opponent off his feet and slamming him to the mat.

Snap-Down: A maneuver in which the opponent is brought

to the mat by seizing him by the neck and arm, stepping backward, unsettling his balance, thus forcing him to the mat.

Spar: When neither wrestler takes a grip on his opponent while they are on their feet in the neutral position.

Spot Fall: When a direct hold taken from a standing position brings an opponent into a fall.

Step-Over: A maneuver in which a wrestler moves his foot to step over the opponent's body to secure another hold.

Switch: A maneuver in which arm leverage is obtained by swinging an arm over the opponent's corresponding arm and catching inside his thigh or under his body with the same hand; he then shifts the buttocks away exerting strong leverage against the opponent's shoulders. If successful, this stunt reverses the wrestler from the defensive to the offensive position.

Take-down: When a wrestler brings his opponent from a standing position to the mat and under control, thus securing the position of advantage.

Three-Quarter Nelson: A hold obtained when behind an opponent who is on the mat. Both hands or arms are locked around the opponent's neck from one side of his body.

Tie-Up: When one wrestler takes a grip on the other while they are on their feet in a neutral position.

Tight Rider: A wrestler who attempts to keep his opponent broken down into a flattened position on the mat by keeping his hips in close to the opponent and forcing him to carry most of his weight.

Time Advantage: A method of scoring in amateur wrestling. When a wrestler secures a position of advantage, he starts to accumulate time—scoring one point for each full minute of net time advantage. No more than two points can be scored by any one wrestler.

Wing: The maneuver of holding the opponent in tight and rolling him over.

Wristlock: A lock on the opponent's wrist.

Start of a match.

1. The Fundamentals of Wrestling

Wrestling is probably the oldest sport known to man. It is also undoubtedly one of the most challenging.

Wrestling is an individual sport, and once a man steps onto the mat to face an opponent, he's on his own. He must make his own decisions and execute them himself.

Though many people think of wrestling as a sport in which the strongest man always wins, this is not necessarily true. Wrestling depends on strength, of course, but it also depends on many other qualities. In fact, a modern amateur wrestling match involves its

participants more thoroughly, perhaps, than any other physical activity.

Wrestling is 6 to 9 minutes (maximum is 3 periods of 3 minutes each) of constant mental and physical exertion, moving with lightning speed, and in the right direction, carrying out strategy in the face of a constantly changing situation. It is one of the most demanding of all sports—and one of the most satisfying. Every

wrestler knows that when he's pinned his man he has done it himself. He has out-thought, out-maneuvered, and outlasted a man of equal ability in a contest of skill. This is wrestling.

Alertness, agility, endurance, strength, skill—all of these qualities and more are involved in wrestling. To get the most out of this sport you have to condition yourself. There are many muscles in your body that will be brought into play only as you wrestle.

The winner's hand is raised in a symbol of victory.

Vigorous calisthenics help get those muscles ready for use, and lessen the chance of injury.

Becoming muscle-bound is not the object of conditioning. You'll need to be quick and precise when you're on the mat in competition. Big, bulging muscles might slow you down. Exercises that perfect your timing, coordination and balance are the best for a wrestler

Conditioning for wrestling consists of following a program of calisthenics to gain suppleness.

Exercises that perfect timing, coordination and balance—plus plenty of sleep— are best for wrestling conditioning.

to practice. And, of course, all the physical activity you do is just so much wasted effort unless you're following a *program* of conditioning. This means you must eat good solid food (cut out sweets) and keep your weight as low as possible all the time; get plenty of regular rest; and work out on schedule.

It also means that you must know what equipment is proper—and how to take care of it. A wrestler's gear is simple; a supporter, shorts, light shoes and, depending on local regulations, a shirt or long pants and a helmet. It's taken for granted that you will keep your gear spotlessly clean and in good condition.

To get the most out of the sport, you should understand the rules and procedures. At the back of this book you will find the official rules for wrestling competition. Read them and remember them. Wrestling is bringing an opponent to the mat from a standing position and maneuvering in such a way as to pin his shoulders to the mat. A match is over when a pin, or fall, is achieved. But very often there is no pin or fall; in this case, whichever wrestler scores more points in the complete session is considered the winner.

A normal match starts from a neutral standing position. First you endeavor to "take down" your opponent, that is, you try to get him down to the mat. Next, you try to "break down" your opponent. This means you want to destroy the effectiveness of his position on the mat and keep him under control—or ride him—until you are ready to try for a fall. Finally, after you are sure you

Neutral standing position.

A takedown.

have control, you want to maneuver your opponent into some kind of a combination of holds that will lead to a pin or fall. There are a great many such pinning combinations and, of course, each one requires a different overall strategy. We will go into this in detail later.

Your procedure in an ideal match would be to move briskly and decisively from the takedown to the breakdown through rides and pinning combinations to the fall. But that presumes that your opponent is just letting you push him around—which is, of course,

A breakdown.

A pinning combination.

far from the case. An alert, skilful opponent will always be trying to *counter* every move you make. In fact, it's the constant attacking and counter-attacking that makes a wrestling match fascinating, exciting and a supreme test of many skills. There is a counter for every maneuver in a wrestling match, and in the photos in this book the proper counter will be shown right after the maneuver itself.

There is another series of maneuvers that has to be given *special* consideration—escapes and reversals. These are the aggressive maneuvers a wrestler can make if he is the underneath man in the

A counter.

16

The underneath man tries to "escape and reverse."

referee's position (see glossary) or in some other defensive situation. An individual with a knowledge of escapes and reversals can gain the upper hand quickly and upset his opponent's plans.

This then is the pattern of a real match: to take down an opponent, break down his mat position, ride and keep him under control until you can pin his shoulders—escaping, reversing, and countering whenever the situation demands it. This procedure may sound complicated but the wrestler who has an over-all strategy usually has the least difficulty winning.

To understand good strategy, let's take a look at how a man moves an object of his own weight—as wrestlers are constantly called upon to do.

The underneath man is about to succeed in his escape and reverse.

The underneath man is in control. He can now use his shoulder as a fulcrum.

Suppose you are faced with the task of moving a crate that weighs as much as you do. You might try shoving it along the floor with your hands. But the crate has a low center of gravity, and it will take a hefty push on your part to move it very far.

If you can shift that center of gravity, the crate will be much easier to move. By putting a plank under one edge of the crate, and using a pile of bricks as a pivot, you can make a *lever* for yourself. With it, you can shift the crate's center of gravity so that now the slightest

push is all you need to topple its heavy weight. With a lever you have had much less work and used much less energy to move the crate. This is applying a basic principle of mechanics: force applied over a fulcrum (the pile of bricks) is more efficient than force applied straight-on. Anybody who has ever used a crowbar can testify to that. In wrestling, you are constantly using the principle

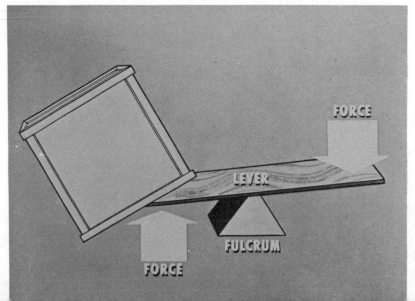

There is a lever being used in both the photos on this page.

of the lever to shift your opponent's center of gravity and make him easier to move. There is a lever being used here.

Finding and using the right levers at the right moment is an important part of a wrestler's skill.

The wrestler on the right is using a lever in this arm-drag takedown.

There is more than one lever being used in this figure-4 scissors pinning combination.

There is a lever being used below—but it is a dangerous one. That's why the full nelson, as this hold is called, is an *illegal* hold. So an understanding of leverages is also important in helping a wrestler avoid illegal holds.

The full nelson— an illegal hold.

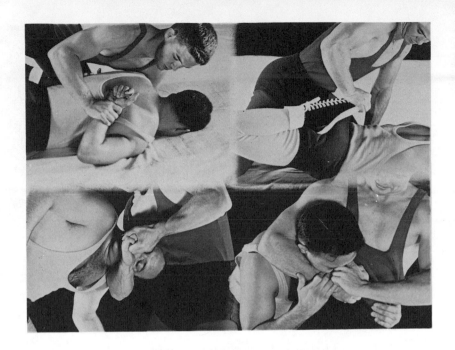

Generally speaking, an illegal hold in wrestling is one which would endanger an opponent's body in any way. The hammer lock (top left) endangers the shoulders, the toe hold (top right) may damage the toe and knee, the twisting front headlock (lower left) can damage the neck, and gouges (lower right), slams and punches have no place in wrestling.

Amateur wrestling survives today because it is a clean, fair sport—depending on skill rather than on brute force and theatrical tactics.

Your footwork is of major importance in wrestling.

2. Takedowns

A wrestling match is a *chain* of maneuvers, and even though most of the activity takes place on the mat, a very important part of your wrestling skill begins with what you do on your feet as you maneuver into the takedown.

Let's begin with the stance and footwork. A wrestler must be sure-footed, nimble, and careful not to let his feet get in his own way. But stance involves much more than footwork alone. It involves balance, timing, and agility.

The open stance is the wrestler's version of sparring. The opponents must keep moving. It gives each man time to size up his op-

ponent, think about his own strategy, anticipate the strategy of his opponent, and be ready to seize the first good opportunity to try for a takedown.

From a sparring position, there are several dependable takedowns. The one we'll discuss first is a single leg dive, or tackle. (It can also be done from a tie-up position.)

Tie-up position.

*Single-leg
dive or
tackle—
Step 1.*

It begins as you dive for your opponent's right leg (Step 1). Circling to his right, you grasp his heel with your right hand (Step 2). Your head should then be outside your opponent's right knee and your left shoulder and left arm should encircle your opponent's waist.

Step 2

Step 3

A little leverage in the right places and you have tripped your opponent to the mat. (Step 3).

But remember, there is a *counter* for every maneuver in wrestling. An alert opponent, sensing that you intend to pull a single leg dive, will immediately begin to counter. He will lift his leg as you come in for the tackle. Then, he will flatten himself out on top of you and apply a downward pressure on your shoulders (Step 1).

Counter to the single-leg dive —Step 1

Step 2

From this position he can then keep his captured leg from being pulled up (Step 2), and, at the same time start a new aggressive maneuver on you.

Now let's look at another kind of takedown that can be made

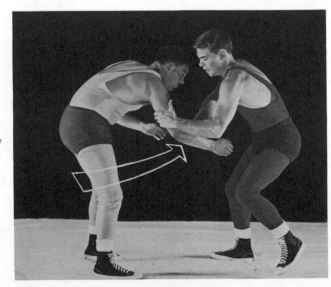

The pull-by —Step 1

Step 2

from a sparring start. This one, called the drag or pull-by, involves pulling your opponent past you and thus forcing him to the mat.

You begin by getting a firm hold on his arm and pull (Steps 1 and 2). You drag him down towards the mat with your right arm (Step 3)—while with your left you grasp his leg behind the thigh

Step 3

(Step 4). You now have good leverage, and can simultaneously pull and swing your opponent around so that you are on top with one leg hooked over his (Step 5). From here, you can go into the breakdown and ride phase of your strategy.

But—suppose he has anticipated your maneuver? He would counter, by grasping your right arm below the shoulder pit, and would drop his weight to his right (Step 1). He now has the better leverage and can pull you past him (Step 2). This maneuver is known as the counter drag, or redrag, and if successful, brings the countering man out on top (Step 3).

Step 5

The counter drag—
Step 1

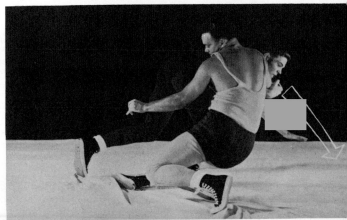

Step 2

Step 3

*The spin
—Step 1.*

Step 2

The spin is a third way to gain a takedown from a sparring position. In a short arm spin you catch your opponent's right arm at the elbow and start to pull him across in front of you (Step 1). At the same time you drop to one knee and grasp your opponent's right ankle. Your head is in front of his leg and your other arm is around his waist (Step 2). With the leverage these grips give you, you can force him to the mat with relative ease.

*The counter spin—
Step 1.*

But let's see what he could have done to counter this spin maneuver. His counter would begin after you had grasped his leg. After grasping your right arm below the shoulder, he would shoot his left arm across to grasp back of your thigh (Step 1), and then begin to drag you past him (Step 2). You must know your counters if you are going to be successful in blocking your opponent's counter.

Step 2

A slightly more common way to work for the takedown is from a tie-up position. This means that instead of sparring, you elect to come to grips with your opponent right away. You "tie up" with him by using your arms.

Another is the collar and triceps tie-up. One arm goes behind your opponent's neck, with your forearm resting on his collarbone area. The other arm goes to his opposite triceps and biceps muscle area.

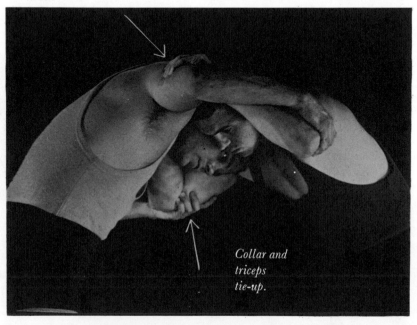

Collar and triceps tie-up.

34

The collar and triceps tie-up lets you keep your feet a good distance from your opponent's feet, yet it puts you in a position to work several types of takedowns.

This is the underarm and triceps tie-up. You work into it by grasping your opponent's right arm with your left hand and you put your right arm under his left armpit.

The underarm and tricepts tie-up also gives your legs protection, yet it still lets you maneuver for the takedown.

Double elbow tie-up.

The double elbow tie-up is a defense for the collar and triceps tie-up position. Starting with that position, grasp your opponent's right elbow with your left hand and grasp his left arm in a similar spot. This maneuver will bring you in and under your opponent.

Now let's go back and take a look at some of the takedowns that can be made from the various tie-up positions. You are locked in the collar and triceps tie-up. How can you get your opponent to the mat? The overhead drag (Step 1) is one good maneuver.

Overhead drag— Step 1.

It begins as you move to your right and then drop on your knees, at the same time keeping your opponent moving with a thrust against his elbow (Step 2). You are "dragging his arm" over your head, spinning him to his left. You keep dragging or turning him as you grasp his right ankle (Step 3). Since most of his weight is on his left foot you can easily pick that right foot up and send him to the mat (Step 4). Easily, that is, if your opponent has not already countered.

Step 4

Drag-and-sit-down maneuver.

The counter is a drag-and-sit-down maneuver. In this case, he would have begun to grasp your right arm as you dropped to your knee. He would then sit down, take hold of your thigh and drag you past him.

Another takedown from the collar and triceps tie-up position is the drag and trip. You begin this drag by rolling your opponent's right arm so as to break his grip on your elbow (Step 1). His right arm is now free to be grasped for the drag.

You catch it with your right hand and start pulling your opponent to your right (Step 2). At the same time, you step in to trip with your right leg behind his (Step 3), forcing him back over your leg

The drag and trip— Step 1.

Step 2

Step 3

with your right arm (the "dragging" arm) against his chest (Step 4).

A re-drag—Step 1.

The drag and trip is open to the same kind of counter as the arm drag, that is . . . a re-drag. Here, your opponent begins the counter just as you trip him (Step 1) by catching your right arm and "dragging" you past him as he falls (Step 2). At the same time his left

Step 2

hand reaches for a rear thigh, and as you both hit the mat he comes
out on top (Step 3). Countering any maneuver, demands agility
speed, and, above all, the awareness of your opponent's intentions.
You should always be ready to apply counters as well as to anticipate
them.

Step 3

*The underarm
sweep—
Step 1.*

The underarm sweep is another takedown maneuver that can be performed from the collar and triceps tie-up. It begins as you lift your opponent's right arm and duck under it (Step 1). Next, drop on one knee and place your left hand behind your opponent's right leg (Step 2). Your right hand is still on his collar. You now have two points at which pressure can be applied to spin your opponent: his crotch and neck. You spin him forward as you pivot on your knee, and he falls toward the mat (Step 3). You can now easily get to his ankle or his arm for a breakdown.

Step 2

Step 3

But, he may counter in one of two ways: by locking your right arm with his and pulling you under in a near-side wing maneuver (Step 1), or by stepping over your knee and forcing you back with his hips (Step 2).

Step 2

Step 1—Double leg tackle—Step 2.

Now suppose you are locked up in the underarm and triceps position. One of the takedowns you can use effectively is the double leg tackle. Begin by dropping quickly to your knees and tackling your opponent around the thighs (Steps 1 and 2). If you move quickly and secure a good grip, your opponent will fall across your shoulder (Step 3). You now go on to the takedown, throwing your left leg forward, and pivoting on your right knee (Step 4), throwing your opponent past you and onto the mat (Step 5). Continue pivot-

Step 3

Step 4

Step 5

ing on your knee until you throw yourself on top of your opponent (Step 6), ready to go into the breakdown and ride phase of your strategy.

Step 6

Countering the double leg dive—Step 1.

But now let's go back and see what your opponent can be expected to do when he realizes you are attempting the double leg dive and takedown. There you are on your knees and ready to throw your left foot forward and begin the pivot (Step 1). You notice that your opponent, instead of just lying across your shoulder as he did before, has flattened himself out and is reaching for your far arm. If he gets it, he can force you to let go of his leg and get a rear crotch hold on you with his other hand (Step 2). Then he can swing behind you (Step 3) and be in a good position to use some other breakdown on you (Steps 4, 5 and 6).

The double leg dive, one of the most popular of takedowns, requires speed, timing, and coordination. You must learn both the maneuver itself and the counter.

Step 2

Step 3

Step 4

Step 5

Step 6

The back heel trip is another method of achieving a takedown
from the underarm and triceps tie-up. It begins as you move to your
left . . . causing your opponent to step forward with his left foot (Step
1). Now then quickly, reverse your direction and drop to your
knee (Step 2). Bring your right hand down behind his right leg and
you now have your opponent in an unbalanced position (Step 3).
By swinging your left arm around and under his leg and applying
pressure with your arm and head, you can achieve a backward trip
(Step 4).

But if you don't get your arm around fast enough, your opponent
will be able to counter. He will throw his hips against yours and put
his body parallel with yours (Step 1). This maneuver, a hiplock
counter leaves your opponent free to force you to the mat with his
hips and shoulders (Step 2).

Step 2

Step 3

48

Step 4

*Hiplock
counter—
Step 1.*

Step 2

49

The crackdown and spin—Step 1.

Step 2

Step 3

Now suppose you find yourself in a collar and triceps tie-up with an opponent. There are at least two good takedown maneuvers from

this position. The first is a crackdown and spin. Drive into your opponent as you drop to your knees, and he will push back (Step 1). His pressure has set him up to be cracked down. So, shove his right arm out from under him (Step 2). As you crack him down, spin him to your right and spin yourself around and on top (Step 3).

Your opponent could counter this maneuver as you start the spin by capturing your left leg with his right arm, as you start around to his right (Step 1). He would then encircle your leg with his own, and trip you onto the mat (Step 2).

Step 2

Step 1—The underarm sweep—Step 2.

The underarm sweep, one of the most popular of takedowns, also begins from a collar and triceps tie-up (Step 1). With a firm grip on his left elbow, you sweep down and under your opponent's right arm (Step 2), and continue sweeping upward and to your left until you are behind your man (Step 3).

Then pull him down with your right arm (Step 4). Your left is free to reach for an inside crotch hold, and thus lead into a breakdown maneuver.

Step 3

Step 4

The underarm sweep may be countered with a hiplock. This would begin as you, the offensive man, sweep around toward your opponent's back. He would windmill his free right arm and grip your right arm (Step 1). Then your opponent would try to pull you up and move his hips back for a good hiplock position (Step 2). In this way he would apply his own leverage to force you to the mat (Step 3).

Countering the underarm sweep—Step 1.

Step 2   *Step 3*

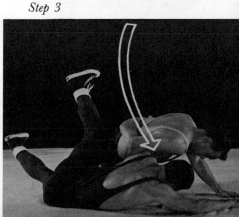

The kind of takedown you choose depends on the kind of starting position you've elected. It's important to know takedowns from all the starting positions, to know where they all lead, and to know how to counter them. Wrestling is a chain of maneuvers and the success or failure of your takedown can easily determine the success or failure of your entire strategy.

3. Breakdowns and Rides

Having control of your opponent is one of the secrets of successful wrestling. With good control you can pursue your strategy the way YOU have planned it, and get your man ready for a fall.

The problem of maintaining control comes up most strongly as soon as you find yourself wrestling on the mat. For your opponent will be constantly trying to escape or to take a position that resists control.

The referee's position.

The *referee's position* is not only an official starting position, it is also one that wrestlers take whenever they want to offer a maximum of inactive resistance on the mat. Note how this position lets a wrestler plant himself solidly and firmly on the mat. He now has a low center of gravity, and he's going to be hard to break down. To break him down, you will have to destroy one or more of his supports—move an arm, for instance. You will have to shift his center of gravity to drive him to the mat.

This breakdown is the bar arm and waist-lock. It begins as you pull your opponent's near arm out from under (Step).

Bar arm and waistlock —Step 1.

He goes to the mat under additional pressure from the arm you have around his waist (Step 2). Now you are in a good position to keep him under control.

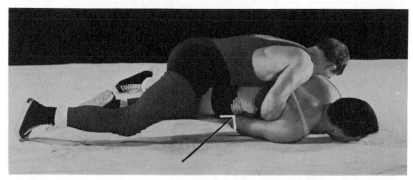

Step 2

But, like every other hold in wrestling, the bar arm and waistlock can be countered with a maneuver, such as the swimmer's break. It is begun after the tie-up position has been reached.

The swimmer's break—Step 1.

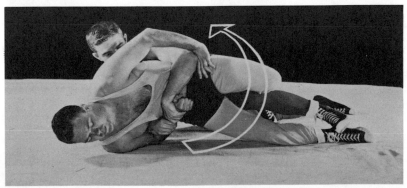

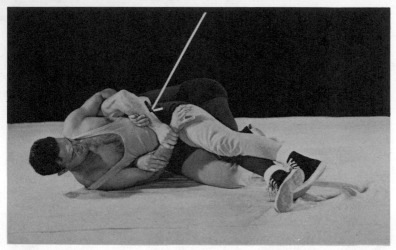

Step 2

To bring it about, your opponent rolls on his side nearest you, laces his left arm over yours and grasps your wrist. (Step 2) The leverage he has there will enable him to snap your grip loose. At the same time it leaves his right hand free. Note that he is in a good position to move into a switch maneuver (Step 3).

Step 3

Another breakdown maneuver from the referee's position is the hip breakdown. It is started as you push your left knee against your opponent's right knee (Step 1). Since your left arm is still around his waist and your right is gripping his at the elbow, you are in a good position to use the combined leverages of your arms and knee to bring your opponent to the mat (Step 2).

*Hip breakdown—
Step 1.*

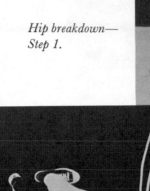

Step 2

If you keep your man well under control, you should now be able to ride him until you can get him into position where you can apply a fall hold.

Fall hold.

Outside switch—Step 1.

But, you must always be prepared for his counter maneuver. As soon as he realizes you are working him into a hip breakdown, he might put an outside switch (Step 1).

An outside switch begins as your opponent rolls towards you (Step 2), snapping his arm free of your grip. Still pivoting away

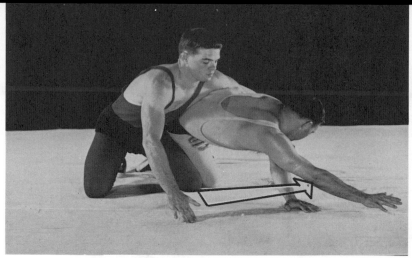

Step 3

(Step 3), he swings completely around (Step 4), reaches for a back crotch position and comes out on top (Step 5). The switch is a reversal maneuver and, as we will see, can be countered too. It's all part of the constant maneuvering that characterizes a good wrestling match.

Step 4

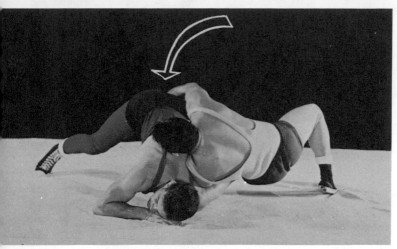

Step 5—Outside switch accomplished.

Another method of breaking a man down from the referee's position is known as the far ankle and far arm. The offensive man is in black. Your first move on the offensive is suddenly to let go of your opponent's near arm (Step 1). Then, shooting your hand under

Step 1—Far ankle and far arm—Step 2.

Step 3

his armpit, grasp his far arm just above the elbow (Step 2). Pulling that far arm under your opponent's chest and reaching for his far ankle with your other hand, sends him to the mat (Step 3), and puts you in a position to apply pressure at 3 important points: on the far ankle, on the far arm, and on your opponent's chest (Step 4). But now, let's go back and see what your opponent might do to keep from getting into this predicament.

Step 4

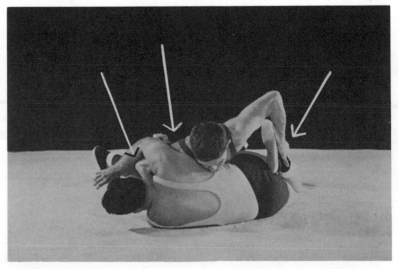

Step 1—Counter to the far arm and ankle breakdown—Step 2.

The counter to the far-arm-and-ankle breakdown depends largely on keeping a man from getting a grip on your far arm (Step 1), and thus keeping your support.

One way your opponent could counter your maneuver would be to shoot his far arm out and away (Step 2) so you can't reach it.

Another counter would allow you to reach your arm across, but then he would take a wing grip on that arm (Step 1), throw his whole weight downward over it and force you down onto your side (Step 2). This wind-down maneuver would position him to step his right leg over your hips, thereby completing a reversal of positions.

Step 1—Wing-down maneuver—Step 2.

Grapevine or cross-body ride—Step 1.

Another ride is the grapevine or cross-body. It requires great speed and agility on the part of the wrestler who wishes to apply it. You would begin it from the referee's position by "climbing" onto your opponent's near leg (Step 1). Then, straightening out, force his right leg to the right and insert your right leg in front of his, and between his legs (Step 2).

Step 2

Step 3

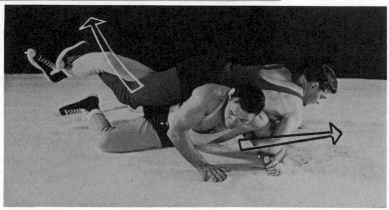

You would improve your position by moving further across his body (Step 3) so that you can reach his far arm and encircle it (Step 4). See how this ride puts you in a position to apply pressure in two directions, forcing your opponent down onto the mat and making it possible for you to get even better control.

Straight front scissors—Step 1.

A variation of the cross-body ride is a breakdown by means of a straight front scissors. From the referee's position you must get on your opponent's back with a lever under each of his table-like supports (Step 1).

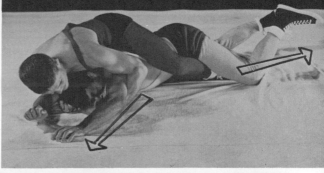

Step 2

Step 3

As you now straighten out, you buckle each of these supports (Step 2), and your opponent goes to the mat—with you in complete control of the situation (Step 3). Countering both the straight front scissors and the cross-body ride begins early in the maneuver.

Counter—Step 1.

As you try to get on top from the referee's position, your opponent would push your knee through *further* than you want it to go (Step 1).

67

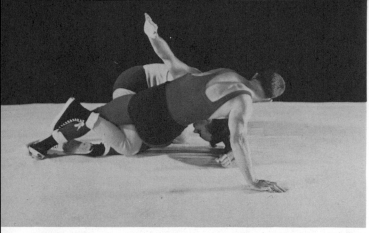

Step 2

This forces you too far forward, and makes it impossible for you to move back on top in a position to maintain your cross-body ride (Step 2). Instead of that you slide off over his shoulder (Step 3). But whichever counter he does use, maintaining control is the object. Controlled wrestling, rather than helter-skelter tumbling and grabbing, is what distinguishes the real performer. And the real performer is the one who gets most satisfaction from the game, win or lose.

Step 3

4. Pinning Combinations

Though pinning a man is not the only way to win a wrestling match, it is one of the most gratifying. Like a knockout, it puts a clean and decisive finish to a match, and in a contest between experts it is most often the result of strategy, planning, and skill—rather than just a stroke of luck. The pin or fall is the final outcome of a well-wrestled chain of maneuvers.

Scoring points.

For scoring purposes points are awarded for takedowns, escapes, reversals, control time, a predicament, and near fall.

A predicament is said to occur in certain situations where the offensive wrestler has control of his opponent in a pinning combination and a near fall or fall is imminent.

PREDICAMENT

NEAR FALL

A near fall is a situation in which the offensive wrestler has control of his opponent in a pinning combination, with both shoulders or the scapula area held in contact with the mat for one full second; or when one shoulder of the defensive wrestler is touching the mat, and the other shoulder, is held within *one inch* or less of the mat, for two full seconds.

A true fall occurs only when both of the opponent's shoulders are held in contact with the mat for the full 2-second count. While the near fall and predicament are important to know about, it is the true fall that will concern us in this chapter.

FALL

There are many pinning combinations possible from each one of the breakdowns that have been illustrated. Let's see what can be done when you have your opponent under control in a bar arm and waistlock breakdown.

In the shoulder roll pinning combination, your inside knee is pressed into your opponent's thigh as you buckle under his near arm (Step 1).

Locking your own hands around him, you pull your opponent toward your hip (Step 2). This turns him up on his shoulders (Step 3).

Shoulder roll— Step 1.

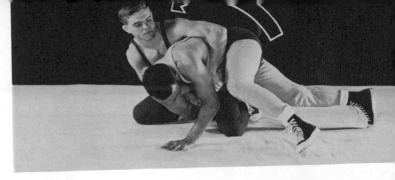

Step 2

Step 3

Then throw your leg across his head, to hold him tight for the pin (Step 4).

Step 4

But now let's see what he might have done to counter this shoulder roll combination. Instead of letting you turn him with your hip, he would have tried to straighten out, and get into a prone position close to the mat. It's easy to see that a shoulder roll pinning combination is impossible if your opponent maintains a low center of gravity like this.

Another common pinning maneuver from the bar arm and waist-

Step 2

Beginning of the bar arm and half-nelson.

lock breakdown is the bar arm and half-nelson. It is begun (above) by stepping your left knee over behind his right leg and forcing him forward, and at the same time, breaking his right arm under to apply a two-hand grip on his wrist (Step 2).

You now move to the left and apply a half-nelson (Step 3). This

Step 2

Step 3

well-known hold gives you excellent leverage on your opponent's neck.

As you start to put on the pressure you pull his head under and move more to the left, and drive him on to his shoulders (Step 4).

By driving right on over him, you can improve your half-nelson so that all you need to do to gain the pin is drive him hard toward the mat (Step 5).

Countering the half-nelson.

But let's look at a counter to this pinning combination. One counter would begin just as you get the half-nelson on your opponent's neck. By keeping his head up and his left shoulder down, and throwing his far leg out to brace himself, he effectively prevents you from applying the pressure of your half-nelson.

Crotch and half-nelson pinning combination—Step 1.

The crotch and half-nelson pinning combination can develop from the back crotch and far arm breakdown. It begins as you take a back crotch with your left hand and shoot your right hand under to grasp your opponent's far arm (Step 1). Pulling that arm underneath, you can drive him on to his left side (Step 2).

Step 2

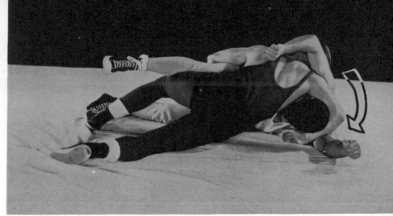

Step 3

If you now get a half-nelson with your right arm (Step 3), and at the same time an inside crotch with your left (Step 4), you're in a good spot to press for a fall. Note how your legs are out of his reach, and how your half-nelson arm almost completely encircles his neck.

Step 4

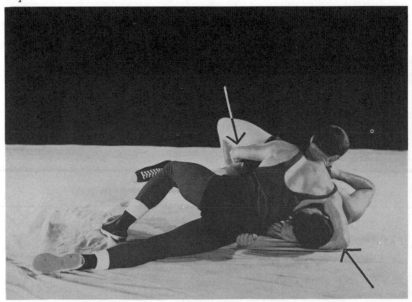

Countering the crotch and half-nelson pin—Step 1.

Your opponent could try to counter here by bridging up and inserting his right hand between your chest and his (Step 1). Falling back to the mat (Step 2), and quickly bridging again (Step 3), he might manage to wedge his arm deeper between your bodies. Then, turning over on his side, he might force his right arm through (Step 4)—allowing him to turn face downward and break up your attempted crotch and half-nelson pinning strategy.

Step 2

Another possible pinning combination from the bar-arm and waistlock breakdown begins as you take a chicken wing on your opponent and begin to cross over his body (Step 1).

Chicken wing and cross-over—Step 1.

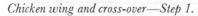

Step 2

Step 3

As you cross over, take a half-nelson on his neck with your left hand (Step 2). The combined pressure of your chicken wing and half-nelson is enough to turn your opponent's head under and bring his shoulder toward the mat. To secure the fall you roll him over further, and secure his head with your knee (Step 4).

Step 4

A successful counter to this pinning combination depends on the elbow. If your opponent can press his winged elbow to the mat (Step 1), he can use it as a pivot, roll all the way over (Step 2), and

Counter —Step 1   *Step 2*

Step 3

come out on top, putting you in a very precarious position (Step 3). This is a good example of how the situation is always changing in a match between two skilled wrestlers.

The chicken wing can be developed into another pinning combination called the figure-4 head scissors. Force your opponent onto his side (Step 1). Then swing your right leg around his head

Figure-4 head scissors—Step 1.

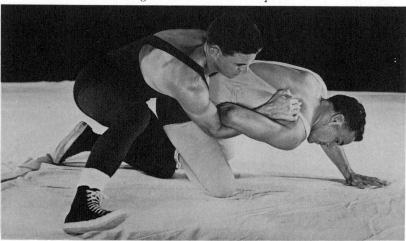

Step 2

Step 3

and hold it in a half-nelson (Step 2). Lock that grip by moving your right foot up so you can hook it over your left leg (Step 3).

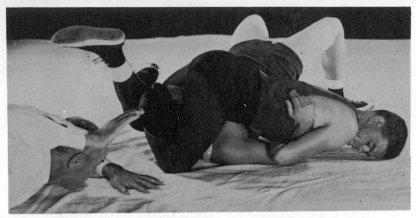

Step 4

Then your legs will resemble a figure 4 (Step 4). You've held onto your chicken wing and now you can push that arm down until your opponent's shoulder goes to the mat, with you clearly on top.

The counter to this maneuver should begin at the chicken wing stage. Your opponent, held in wing lock (Step 1), would straighten his winged arm—breaking your grip and making it impossible for you to continue the figure-4 scissors maneuver (Step 2).

Step 1—Counter to figure-4 head scissors—Step 2.

Now let's go back to the hip breakdown and see what pinning combinations can be developed from it. You will remember that a hip breakdown involves forcing your opponent to the mat on his side nearest you. Lace your left arm between your opponent's legs (Step 1) and pull up on one leg (Step 2).

Lace-ride combination —Step 1.

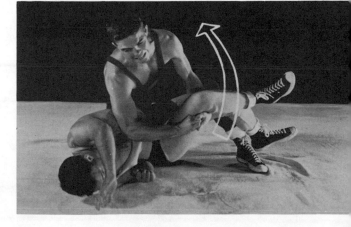

Step 2

This will force your opponent in a cradle-fall hold (Step 3).

To counter this lace-ride combination your opponent would begin by pushing your head down (Step 1). Step his right leg over your head and turn towards the mat (Step 2).

Counter to lace-ride combination—Step 1.

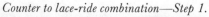

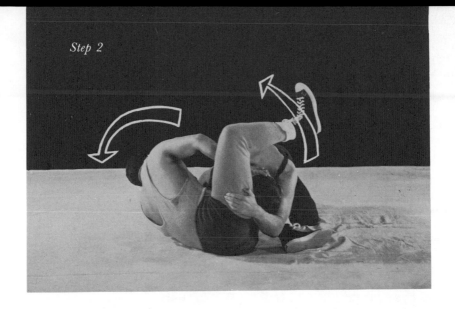

The cradle pin can be developed from this far-ankle and cross-face ride (Step 1). Pull up on your opponent's left foot and apply the cross-face pressure.

Cradle pin— Step 1.

Step 2

This will force him to drop to his right hip. He is now in position for you to apply a back crotch (Step 2). But retain the cross-face grip until you can join your own hands and get ready to pull your opponent backwards (Step 3). Doing so, you have him in a cradle, and when you hook your leg around his free leg (Step 4), you have him in a situation which is almost sure to result in a fall. Once in this position, there is little chance for an effective counter.

Step 3

Reverse half-nelson.

Now let's see what pinning combinations follow from the cross-body ride. The reverse half-nelson is one. From a cross-body position (Step 1), you capture your opponent's left arm and lift it over your own head (Step 2).

Step 1

Step 2

Now lie back and your whole body becomes a powerful lever (Step 3), that can hardly fail to throw your opponent's shoulders to the mat (Step 4). By locking your hands together (Step 5), you can put on that final burst of pressure that will give you the fall.

Step 4

Step 5

The counter to the reverse half-nelson begins as you try to capture that left arm (Step 1). By sliding it away and at the same time rolling

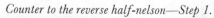

Counter to the reverse half-nelson—Step 1.

Step 2

Step 3

you over with his hips (Step 2), your opponent can snap his arm free (Step 3), thereby escaping from the possible reverse half-nelson position.

Double-trouble pinning combination.

The more you understand about the chain of maneuvers, such as the double-trouble pinning combination (above), the better you will be able to make your strategy work, your knowledge of levers pay off, and your pinning combinations do their job.

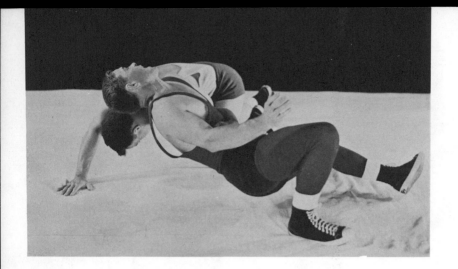

5. Escapes and Reverses

We've seen that, in wrestling, a counter is an attempt to prevent an opponent from executing a maneuver. But sometimes even the best-planned counter will not work. You then find yourself held in control—on the defensive.

Your only way of gaining the offensive is to escape or reverse positions. A wrestler whose escape and reversal strategy is effective cannot easily be pinned, because he cannot be held under control. Since most escapes are executed from underneath, they are illustrated here from the referee's position, where one man is clearly on the defensive. Escapes and reverses can be made, however, from almost any defensive position.

We've seen how the switch works as a counter. Now let's see how it functions as a reversal maneuver. Take the outside switch first. You begin by pivoting on your knee (Step 1), and step through with

The referee's position.

Outside switch—Step 1.

Step 2

your right foot into a sitting position, trying to keep your hips off the mat (Step 2). Reach over your opponent's left arm and take a grip on his inside thigh with your left hand. By rearing back you apply pressure back of his left shoulder (Step 3).

Step 3

Step 4

Continue the pressure back of his shoulder and start reaching for a back crotch hold (Step 4). Step back through with your left foot and turn facing your opponent (Step 5). In other words, you not only have escaped, you have reversed your positions.

Step 5

99

Preventing a pivot—Step 1.

Escapes and reverses can be countered just as other maneuvers. To counter a switch, your opponent would reach for your right arm just as you pivot (Step 1). If he can get it, he can pull it under you, destroying your main support, and preventing your pivot (Step 2).

Step 2

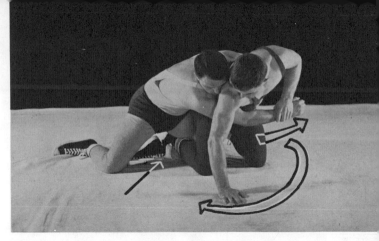

Inside switch—Step 1.

In the referee's position, when your opponent has your near leg hooked, an inside switch is the escape to use. Grasp his right wrist with your left hand and pull his arm under (Step 1). Set your left foot through and turn on your back (Step 2). Reach for an inside crotch hold with your right hand, then rear back against his right

Step 2

Step 3

shoulder, then turn over and take a back crotch hold with your
left (Step 3). The inside switch is now complete, and is actually a
reverse, since you are now in the position of advantage.

But, your opponent could counter by pulling a reswitch on you.
The counter reswitch begins as you start to come around behind
him (Step 1).

Counter reswitch—Step 1.

Step 2

Your opponent shoots his left foot under you, supporting himself with his left arm (Step 2). He then sets his left leg through, turning you over in the process (Step 3). Continuing in the same direction, with the pressure of his right arm back of your right shoulder, he gets a rear crotch hold on you and tries to drive you forward and

Step 3

Step 4

to the mat (Step 4). He has countered your switch with one of his own, and retained control over you at the same time.

In a power switch, you set your leg through just as in a regular inside switch, hooking the in-step of your right foot against the inside of the thigh of his right leg (Step 1). By extending that leg,

Power switch— Step 1.

Step 2

scooting your hips to one side, and pushing back with your shoulder (Step 2), you put your opponent off balance . . . so that you can get a rear crotch hold (Step 3). You improve this position by stepping back through with your left leg (Step 4). You have completed the reversal.

Step 4

105

Your opponent's counter would begin as you set through and hook his leg. If he can move to his right he would step his right leg over (Step 1), making your hook and extension of the leg ineffective (Step 2).

The set-out is another kind of escape maneuver that will bring you out from under. Starting from the referee's position, you step

Step 2

*Set-out
maneuver
—Step 1.*

your right foot forward first (Step 1). Then, shoot your left foot out and drop on your left side (Step 2). Step 3 shows the basic set-out maneuver, in which you have "set yourself out in front" of your opponent.

Step 2

Step 3

Step 4

Now you pivot on your left shoulder, roll over, and jerk yourself free of your opponent (Step 4). You've escaped, and are now ready to grapple again from a neutral position (Step 5).

Step 5

*Bar arm
counter—
Step 1.*

But if your opponent has seen that escape coming, he will have
tried to counter it. The bar arm counter would begin as you try to
fall onto your left side. Your opponent would break your left arm
support down (Step 1) and drive his right shoulder into you, forcing
you to your left side (Step 2).

Step 2

Step 1—Variation of the set-out—Step 2.

In this variation of the set-out, you begin with the standard maneuver—shooting your feet out one at a time (Step 1). But instead of pivoting, you first catch your opponent's head with your right arm (Step 2). Now you drop and begin to pivot (Step 3). As you turn under you pull your opponent's head forward and down (Step 4), and you end up with a firm half-nelson around his

Step 3

Step 4

Step 5

head (Step 5). Putting the pressure of that half-nelson to work, you can roll him over and go into one of the pinning combinations—in this case, probably the crotch and half-nelson (Step 6).

Step 6—The crotch and half-nelson.

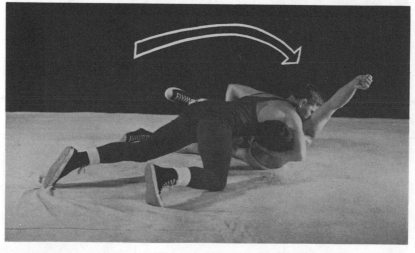

Now let's go back and see where your opponent would begin a counter. As you drop down from your set-out maneuver, he would bring his right arm up under your right arm pit (Step 1). With his other hand he would grasp your chin (Step 2). Now, with both

Step 2

Step 3

hands, he would try to pull you back onto the mat for a possible fall (Step 3).

The roll is another kind of escape. From the referee's position, the side roll, one variation, begins as you grasp your opponent's underneath wrist (Step 1), and straighten your left leg. Keeping

The side roll—Step 1.

*The side roll—
Step 2.*

Step 3

Step 4

114

Step 5

hold of that wrist, you start to drop your elbow to the mat (Step 2).

Drop your right knee out from under you, pivot on your elbow and hip (Step 3), and throw your opponent back over your other hip (Step 4). Hold on to that wrist until you can roll him on over, so that, seen from the other side, you are in a good position to move into a pinning combination (Step 5).

The counter to the side roll would begin as you start dropping to your side. Your opponent would drop his weight back and flatten out, preventing your roll and keeping him on top, in an offensive position.

Counter to the side roll.

Step 1—Inside roll—Step 2.

Another roll escape is the inside roll. It begins as you grasp your opponent's left wrist—the one he has on your bar arm—and pull it under you (Step 1), forcing your opponent's left shoulder to the mat. You roll with him to your left side (Step 2), then you step your left leg over him (Step 3). From this position you can move into a straight-front scissors pinning combination.

Step 3

Step 1—Countering the inside roll—Step 2.

To counter the inside roll, your opponent would try to encircle your trunk with his arms as you start to roll (Step 1). If, at the same time, he can hook your leg with his, he is in a position to continue rolling to his left, and would come back to the position of advantage (Step 2).

One more important group of escapes you should be familiar with are the hiplocks. In general, a hiplock involves some pressure with the hips in an effort to turn or unbalance an opponent. In the windmill hiplock escape . . . you throw your left arm up, over, and around your opponent's waistlock arm (Step 1).

Windmill hiplock escape— Step 1.

By applying forward pressure in back of his right arm, and crowding your hips into his, your downward pressure in back of his shoulder will force him to roll to his left side (Step 2). You can roll him over with your hips and arm (Step 3), forcing him to his left side with his right arm barred (Step 4), and lock him up for a possible fall (Step 5).

Step 3   *Step 4*

Step 5

The counter for the windmill begins early in the maneuver. As soon as your opponent realizes the force of your pressure back of his right arm, he releases his waistlock arm (Step 1), and begins to windmill it. He lets it slide off your left side and thrusts it forward

Countering the windmill —Step 1.

(Step 2), and around so that he has you in a position equivalent to the referee's position (Step 3).

Now you are going to escape by using a quarter-nelson variation of the hiplock. You windmill your inside arm as before, rise, and with your outside hand push your opponent's head down (Step 1), and apply a quarter-nelson. Note how your left wrist is locked on your own right to make this hold work (Step 2). With the leverage you get from this hold you slowly press your opponent's head under and force him to roll on his back (Step 3). By moving to your right you will be in back of your opponent. Here you are in a good position to apply a cradle pinning combination.

Quarter-nelson variation of the hiplock —Step 1.

Step 2

Step 3

Step 1—Double trouble—Step 2.

Your opponent might try to counter this with a maneuver known as a double trouble. After you have windmilled your inside arm (Step 1), he would quickly throw his outside arm behind your head, and lock his hands (Step 2). The leverage he now has on you will let him bend your head under and double you up (Step 3). This double-trouble counter is a good illustration of how an attempted escape—your quarter-nelson—can be foiled and turned into an advantage that could end the match—in your opponent's favor.

Step 3

Step 1—Hiplock escape or pancake—Step 2.

A final version of the hiplock escape that we will consider is known as the pancake. From a defensive position, you begin with the usual windmill of your inside arm. You apply sufficient pressure back of your opponent's right shoulder to force him to start straightening up (Step 1). Then, you pivot on one knee and with considerable speed and force, shoot your right arm up and under your opponent's left shoulder (Step 2). You follow up by pancaking him over on his back (Step 3).

Step 3

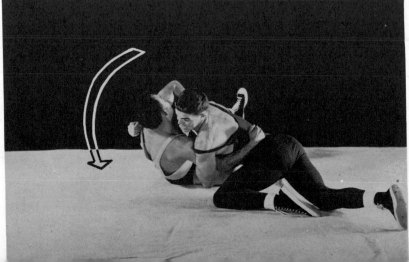

You are now in a good position to effect a double arm tie-up pinning combination (Step 4).

But the pancake, like all other escapes . . . can be countered. Your opponent would choose the moment when you start to pancake (Step 1), and try to lock his arms behind you (Step 2). He would

Countering the pancake.
Step 1

Step 2

124

Step 3

then throw you to the side with a hip-lock motion (Step 3), and drive you on down to the mat (Step 4).

Step 4

There are many more escapes and reverse maneuvers than the basic ones we've illustrated here. That's because an almost unlimited number of situations are possible when two men grapple freely in a clean, open contest. But that's what makes wrestling the exciting and challenging sport of is. For the more you know about possible situations and maneuvers, the better your chances of competing successfully and getting the most out of your wrestling career.

6. Wrestling Rules

These rules are excerpts from the official A.A.U. Wrestling Guide and are reprinted with permission of the Amateur Athletic Union of the United States.

Greco-Roman and Freestyle Wrestling Rules

Article 1 — The definitions contained in the International Wrestling Rules shall be applicable to all Olympic Games Competitions, World Championships, Continental Championships, international and regional competitions and to all international meetings. These definitions of the International Rules shall likewise be applicable to all competitions organised by National Federations which are Members of the International Amateur Wrestling Federation.

Weight Classes

Article 2 — International weight classes for Olympic Games Competitions, World Championships and international matches shall be as follows:

1. Up to 52 Kilos (114.5 lbs.)
2. Up to 57 " (125.5 lbs.)
3. Up to 63 " (138.5 lbs.)
4. Up to 70 " (154 lbs.)
5. Up to 78 " (171.5 lbs.)
6. Up to 87 " (191.5 lbs.)
7. Up to 97 " (213.5 lbs.)
8. Over 97 "

A competitor may compete in one class only, i.e. in the one corresponding to his own bodily weight at the time of the official weighing in, in any one competition.

The final list of competitors shall necessarily be handed in before the weighing-in, in conformity with the regulations in force.

Article 3 — On the first day of a competition, the weighing-in shall begin four hours before and end three hours before the first bout. On the following days, this formality shall begin two hours before and end one hour before the first bout.

In the case of competitions in which the number of contestants is more than 150, the International Technical Committee may alter the times for the weighing-in, the drawing of lots and the pairing-off.

In the case of competitions in which the programme lasts for several days, contestants shall be weighed each day. Wrestlers who have fought their last bouts one day before the end of the competition shall not be weighed on the last day, this to apply to all weight classes.

Competitors shall be weighed in nude and, before the weighing-in, shall be examined by doctors (one of whom shall be the doctor appointed by the organizing country); the latter shall refuse all those who present any danger of contamination. Competitors must be in satisfactory physical condition.

Their nails shall be cut very short and shall be examined at the weighing-in.

Until the end of the weighing-in, competitors shall have the right to get on the scales as many times as they wish, but each in his turn.

DRAWING OF LOTS — PAIRING OFF

Article 4 — The contestants taking part in the competition shall be paired off for each round according to an order number obtained by the drawing of lots.

Article 5 — A form of procedure and a timetable for the events shall be drawn up. The pairing-off for each round, and likewise the results of the rounds, shall be recorded on a list intended for the competitors and the latter shall be entitled to consult it at any time.

Those competitors who have been drawn one after the other shall wrestle against each other in the first round. Should there be an odd number of competitors, the one who draws the highest number shall receive a bye into the next round, without any bad mark being awarded, and he shall then be the first on the list in the pairing-off for this round. He shall keep his place until another competitor becomes the odd man in the same way and then the one with the highest number next to his own shall be placed in front of him.

The right to receive a bye is a right which is acquired by the drawing of lots. It may only be withdrawn in the event of it being impossible for the other competitors to be paired off on account of this right to receive a bye.

The pairing off for the other rounds shall be effected as follows:

The first name to be taken shall be that of the competitor at the top of the list and his opponent shall be the competitor whose name is nearest to his own and who has not yet wrestled against him.

For example: for the second round, should there have been no bye in the previous round: 1-3, 2-4, 5-7, 6-8, etc. Should there have been a bye: The Bye with No. 1, 2-3, 4-5, etc., and so on in the following rounds. In the second round, when there are only six contestants still in the competition, or again when there are only six contestants left to be paired off at the end of the list (for example 10 wrestlers), the following pairings shall be adopted: 1 versus 3, 2 versus 5, 4 versus 6 (when there are 6 competitors) and 1 versus 3, 2 versus 4, 5 versus 7, 6 versus 9 and 8 versus 10 (when there are 10 competitors).

Two competitors from one and the same country shall be matched against each other in the very first round in International Tournaments if they are drawn against each other as a result of the pairing-off.

DRESS

Article 6 — Competitors shall appear before the public in a one-piece singlet and under this they shall wear a truss or a suspender belt.

The singlet shall be tight-fitting and shall cover the body from the middle of the thighs upward; it shall not be cut away by more than two palm-widths around the neck and arms.

The use of light knee-guards shall be permitted.

Nothing whatsoever may be added to this dress, save in the event of a stoppage of the bout on account of injury or for any other reason, when the wrestlers may cover themselves with a warm garment.

The use of shoes with heels or with nailed soles shall be forbidden; contestants shall likewise be forbidden to cover their bodies with greasy or sticky products and they shall not be in a perspiring condition.

No bandages shall be allowed on the wrists, arms or ankles, save in the case of injury and on the doctor's prescription.

The wearing of rings, bracelets, buckle-type shoes and all objects liable to injure an opponent shall likewise be forbidden.

Each competitor shall be freshly shaven at the time of the weighing-in.

Each competitor shall be provided with a handkershief.

Each competitor shall be given two anklets with a width of 10 centimetres and of the color attributed to him (red or green). Competitors shall be forbidden to wear shoes, socks and laces colored green or red or with a color close to green or red.

THE MAT

Article 7 — A mat measuring at least 6 metres by 6 metres along the sides and with a minimum thickness of 10 centimetres shall be compulsory in all international competitions, save in those cases in which the thickness is made up for by a suppleness corresponding to the standards laid down; in such cases, the mat itself may be thinner.

Example: A mat made of a plastic material or of foam rubber.

For Olympic Competitions and World Championships, bouts shall be staged on a mat measuring 8 metres by 8 metres.

In order to avoid all accidents, a free space two metres wide must be left around the mat.

This free space shall be covered with padding of the same, or approximately the same, thickness as the mat itself over 1.20 metres of its width, the remaining area consisting of a clear space 0.80 metres wide (floor of the platform).

The corners of the mat shall be marked with the colors red and green.

The mat shall be fitted on to a raised platform (corner-posts and ropes, as used for boxing rings, are forbidden). The height of the platform shall not exceed 1.10 metres.

Should the mat be installed on a podium and should the protective margin, padding and clear space around the mat not cover a total width of 2 metres, the sides of the podium shall be fitted with panels inclined at an angle of 45°. The protective padding shall in all cases be of a different color; it shall not form part of the mat. Should the combat area be delimited by means of a line, this shall not form part of the regulation mat.

The floor near the mat shall be fitted with a soft covering which shall be carefully fixed in position. The mat shall be covered with a canvas sheet which, in order to avoid all contamination, shall be washed and disinfected; the fastenings on this canvas sheet shall be protected. The mat shall be so positioned as to ensure that a bridge may be made even if the legs are outside.

A circle with an inside diameter of one metre and a circumference width of 10 centimetres shall be marked out in the middle of the mat in a color different from that of the mat itself. The edge of the mat shall likewise be in a different color.

MEDICAL SERVICE

Article 8 — While the competitors are being weighed in, the doctors shall proceed with the medical examination. Should the doctors find that a competitor is not in a good condition of health, he shall not be allowed to take part in the competitions.

No competitor who shows signs of organic deficiency, functional disorders or any other signs which involve a danger to his health or to that of his prospective opponents may take part in the competitions until an opinion has been expressed by the doctor.

A medical service, under the control of a doctor, shall be available throughout the whole duration of the competition and shall be ready to take action in the event of an accident.

The Organizer of the competitions shall in all cases assume the control of the medical service and of the medical assistants. The doctors of the teams taking part shall be entitled, by full right, to intervene with regard to the attention to be given to injured members of their own teams, and likewise in other cases should they have been invited to do so by the official doctor.

The medical service provided at international competitions shall be assured by the official doctor and he alone shall be competent to decide whether a competitor is in a good state of health and may continue the combat, whether his functional limitations form no obstacle to his participation and whether he may continue the combat in the event of injury.

The contestant shall under no circumstances leave the podium.

The trainer and one official of the team may alone be present while attention is being given by the doctor.

In the event of a dispute arising with regard to the medical opinion, the final decision shall be given by the chief doctor, or by the Board of three doctors, should such a Board have been formed. In this last-mentioned case, the doctor for the team of the wrestler in question shall be included in the Board.

Should a competitor be considered to be unfit for the following bouts, this decision shall be valid only after the consultation of the chief doctor or of the Board of three doctors present, together with the doctor of the country to which the injured wrestler belongs, this doctor being given priority. A report shall be drawn up on the accident and this shall be signed by the chief doctor or the Board of doctors.

REFEREE, JUDGES AND ADJUDICATION BOARD

Article 9 — In pursuance of the Regulations of the Technical Committee and the Regulations for the Organization of Competitions, an Adjudication Board shall be set up for each competition; it shall carry out its duties in pursuance of the said Regulations.

Article 10 — In all international competitions, the officials for each bout shall consist of one Mat Chairman, one referee, three judges and three members of the Adjudication Board.

The changing of judges and members of the Adjudication Board during a bout shall be forbidden.

In order to avoid all partiality, compatriots of the competitors may not form part of the Adjudication Board or be judges; the same shall apply in the case of the referee.

There may not be two judges of the same nationality for one and the same bout.

The referee shall be responsible for the evolution of the bout, which he shall control in conformity with the rules. The bout shall start, be interrupted and end when he blows his whistle. He alone shall be authorized, after consulting the judges, to give cautions. He alone shall order the wrestlers to return to the mat should they have left it, or order the bout to be continued in the standing position or on the ground, with the respective opponents in the on-top or underneath positions, this with the approval of the majority of the judges.

The referee and the judges shall be dressed in white and they shall wear the badges of their countries.

The judges and referee shall assume all the duties, prerogatives and responsibilities provided for in the rules for international wrestling competitions, by the interpretations included in this Appendix, by the Regulations of the Technical Committee and by the Regulations for the Organization of Competitions.

It shall be the duty of the referee and the judges to follow the bout with attention, from beginning to end, and to judge the actions in such a way as to ensure that the result shown on their forms shall exactly reflect their general impressions.

The duties, prerogatives and responsibilites of the judges shall also be as follows:

General Duties, Prerogatives and Responsibilities

a) — Should a bout not end in a fall, the decision shall be given by the judges, who shall base themselves on an overall appreciation of all the actions of each of the opponents. For this purpose, a note shall be kept on the judges' forms of all the actions made during the bout, from beginning to end.

b) — The judges' forms shall serve for the awarding of points for all the holds made by both opponents: the points shall be marked down in the sections corresponding to the different stages of the bout.

These notes must be made accurately, the judges form being considered to be the official record of the bout, under the responsibility of the signatory judges.

c) — To assume all duties, prerogatives and responsibilities with regard to the refereeing and the judging, to award the points and to impose the penalties provided for in the International Rules and the Appendix to these Regulations.

All the points awarded by the judges must be made known to the public either by means of bats or by means of luminous plaques.

Special Duties, Prerogatives and Responsibilities

a) — The referee shall control the bout without making any untimely interventions. Should the wrestlers come near the edge of the mat, he must be ready to blow his whistle in pursuance of the regulations.

b) — The referee shall interrupt the bout exactly at the required moment, i.e. neither too early nor too late.

c) — The referee must be familiar with the principle on which to decide whether or not the wrestlers are to be sent back to the inside of the mat and which position he should have them take.

d) — The referee shall not take up a position close to the wrestlers when they are standing, since this would prevent him from watching their legs, but when wrestling is taking place on the ground, he may position himself close to the contestants.

e) — When he sends the wrestlers back to the middle of the mat, the referee shall, without hesitation, give instructions regarding the position in which the wrestling is to be resumed, i.e. in the standing position or on the ground.

f) — Should there be any likelihood of a fall, the referee shall not position himself too close to the wrestlers, this so as not to impede the view of the judges and public.

g) — The referee shall cause himself to be respected by the contestants and shall exercise full authority over them, in order that they shall immediately comply with his orders and instructions.

h) — The referee shall ensure that the wrestlers do not rest during the bout, under the pretense of wiping themselvs, clearing their noses, tying their shoe laces, rinsing out their mouths or by feigning to be injured.

i) — In such cases, the referee shall stop the bout and make a sign to the timekeeper; the bout shall be restarted by the blowing of the referee's whistle.

j) — The referee may, however, give cautions for infringements of the rules or for unnecessary roughness, or should one of the wrestlers refuse to give combat, even at the start of the bout.

k) — The referee must be able to change his position on the mat, or around the mat, at any moment. His clothing must be practical, so that he may instantaneously lie flat on his stomach in order to secure a better view of an impending fall.

l) — The referee shall oblige the wrestlers to remain on the mat until the result has been announced.

m) — In Greco-Roman wrestling, the referee shall watch the wrestlers' legs.

n) — Should the judges notice anything, in the course of the bout, which they consider they should bring to the knowledge of the referee, in the event of the latter not having seen it for himself (a fall, a foul hold, etc.), they shall do this by holding up the bat with the colour corresponding to that of the winner of the wrestler at fault, even if the referee has not asked for their opinion.

o) — The judges and the referee must always be prepared to state the reasons for their decisions whenever requested to do so by the Mat Chairman.

p) — In order to avoid any loss of time, the scoring forms must be signed by the persons concerned as soon as they are received. After the bout, the name of the loser shall be crossed out distinctly on the form.

q) — It is strictly forbidden for the judges and the referee to speak to anyone whatsoever during the bout, with the exception of the Mat Chairman.

r) — The referee shall count each second of a placing in danger by the movement of his arm.

s) — The referee shall always indicate whether a hold that has just been applied at the edge of the mat is valid or not.

t) — In the event of a caution being given, he shall hold the hand of the wrestler at fault.

u) — Before consulting the Adjudication Board, the referee shall in every case first ask for the opinion of the judges stationed by the edge of the mat.

Decisions of the Referee and Judges

a) — The decisions of the judges shall be valid, without any participation of the Adjudication Board, if they are unanimous.

b) — Concerning a fall: a fall shall be clearly indicated; the referee must make certain that a fall has occurred before blowing his whistle.

Disputed Cases

Joint Decisions with the Adjudication Board

The Adjudication Board shall exercise its duties, prerogatives and responsibilities in pursuance of the definitions contained in the International Rules, the Appendix to these Regulations, the Regulations of the Technical Committee and the Regulations for the Organization of Competitions. The Adjudication Board shall take part in the awarding of points.

If the Decision of the Judges is Not Unanimous

The Mat Chairman shall retain all the scoring forms and, after examining them, shall consider them together with the judges' forms in order to arrive at his decision.

The Technical Committee shall be entitled to take the following disciplinary measures against any judge or referee who is at fault:

— a. Give a caution.
— b. Withdraw the offender from the competition.
— c. Declare him to be suspended for a certain time.
— d. Pronounce him struck off the roll.

The I.A.W.F. delegate at international competitions shall be entitled to take the following measures against a referee who is at fault:

— a. Give a caution.

— b. Withdraw him from the competition and subsequently inform the Technical Committee of the I.A.W.A. so that it may make a final decision with regard to his case.

The Start and Duration of the Bouts

Article 11 — For both styles of wrestling, the bout shall be divided into three periods of 3 minutes each with breaks of one minute after the first and second periods.

Whenever a contestant endeavors to hold up the contest (by lacing his shoes, going off the mat, etc.), the referee shall ask for the timing device to be stopped.

The referee alone, acting upon his own conviction, shall be entitled to cause the timing device to be stopped or to stop the bout. The timing device shall be stopped automatically by the timekeeper whenever the referee, by the blowing of his whistle indicates that the action has stopped, either because the wrestlers have gone off the mat, or for any other reason.

The timekeeper shall resume timing the bout when the referee so indicates by the blowing of his whistle.

Each bout shall last until the opponent has been defeated. If this defeat occurs before the elapse of the maximum time laid down, a win shall be recorded, to be counted as a fall, and the bout shall thereupon end.

The timekeeper shall call out the times in a loud voice every minute, in French, English and the language of the organizing country.

Article 12 — Should a competitor fail to put in an appearance on the mat after his name has been duly called, he shall be considered as having lost by a fall and shall be eliminated from the entire competition.

A tolerance period of five minutes shall be allowed in the case of acceptable reasons, **but this only for the first bout in the first round for each class.**

Before the bout, the opponents shall take up their positions in opposite corners of the mat; the referee shall place himself in the middle of the mat and shall call the two wrestlers to his side in order to examine their dress and to verify the fact that they are not covered with any greasy or sticky product and that their hands are bare.

The wrestlers shall greet each other, shake hands and then go to their respective places, each place being marked in the same colour as that of the anklet already given to each contestant and which they must necessarily keep on until the result of the bout has been announced. When the referee blows his whistle, the two wrestlers come together and start wrestling immediately. They do not have to shake hands again until the end of the bout.

Article 13 — A bout may begin, be interrupted or end only on the blowing of the referee's whistle. No competitor shall be entitled to decide for himself that his opponent shall be sent back from the edge of the mat to the middle.

End of the period

Article 14 — At the end of each period, both wrestlers shall be sent back to their respective corners.

Article 15 — Each period shall end after three minutes, regardless of the wrestlers' position. In the event of a placing in danger, the attacking wrestler shall be awarded 2 points if the position lasts for less than 5 seconds and 3 points if the position lasts for 5 or more than 5 seconds.

Article 16 — During the one minute's break, the contestants' trainers and masseurs shall be entitled to come to the edge of the mat. (They shall necessarily be wearing a uniform).

The trainers shall be obliged to leave the mat five seconds before the sounding of the gong.

The sounding of the gong shall indicate the end of the one minute's break in the bout.

The referee shall then call the wrestlers to the middle of the mat to verify that they have been properly wiped down.

A further stroke of the gong, made after the referee has given the sign, shall indicate the beginning of the next period of the bout.

During the one minute's break in the bout, the wrestlers may if they so wish remain standing in their corners or may sit on a small stool placed at a maximum distance of 50 centimetres from the mat. The wrestlers shall be entitled to ask for massage during this period and to receive instruction from their trainers.

Trainers may use towels to wipe down their contestants.

It is forbidden for any dope to be given to a wrestler in order to enable him to recover his strength.

The referee shall necessarily keep a watch on the activities of the trainers and masseurs during the break in the bout.

A trainer may not give instructions to his contestant during the bout; he shall be entitled to stand at the foot of the podium.

The referee shall be bound to give a warning against any infringement of these arrangements.

The Mat Chairman shall be entitled to disqualify a trainer for such infringements and, should the offense be repeated, to disqualify the trainer for the whole duration of the competition. Should his trainer be disqualified, the contestant in question shall be entitled to demand another trainer.

Article 17 — Each period shall always begin with the wrestlers in standing position, regardless of the position of the wrestlers at the end of the previous period.

Wrestling on the Edge of the Mat

Article 18

Standing

a) — Should 3 feet be outside the mat, the bout shall be interrupted and the wrestlers brought back to the middle of the mat to continue wrestling in the standing position.

b) — During the taking of a hold, both feet of one opponent may go outside the mat but the wrestler on the mat shall be allowed to complete his action; the referee shall blow his whistle as soon as the action has been completed.

c) — A wrestler who is outside the mat may no longer apply a hold even if his opponent is still on the mat.

d) — Should both wrestlers leave the mat together, the referee shall order them to return to the position on the mat in which they were before, either standing or on the ground, at the moment they crossed the edge of the mat.

e) — In the case of a bringing down to the ground which is not maintained and which results in both wrestlers leaving the mat, the bout shall be restarted in the middle of the mat in the standing position.

Likewise in the case of a bringing down to the ground, if both hands go beyond the limits, the bout shall be restarted in the standing position.

f) — It shall be considered that three feet are outside if the feet of the wrestler who is lifted are both outside of the mat and if the wrestler who is applying the hold places one of his feet outside the mat.
g) — To be valid, a hold must bring the head and the shoulders within the limits of the mat.

On the ground

a) — Should the wrestler who is underneath be inside the mat (even if 3 or 4 feet are outside), the bout shall be continued so long as the wrestling continues to be inside.

b) — Should the wrestler who is underneath apply a hold which brings both himself and his opponent off the mat, the bout shall be interrupted. Wrestling shall then start again in the standing position in the middle of the mat.

c) — Should the head of the wrestler who is underneath, together with his hands and shoulders, go outside of the mat, the bout shall be stopped.

d) — Should both hands of the wrestler who is underneath touch the floor outside of the mat as a result of an attack, the bout shall be interrupted and the wrestlers brought back to the middle in the kneeling position.

e) — Should the opponent's arms go outside of the mat as the result of a hold, the bout shall be resumed in the standing position. But, should his arms and hands have touched the mat, inside the limits, before going outside, the bout shall be resumed on the ground.

On the Ground Wrestling

Article 19 — If one of the wrestlers is brought down to the ground during the bout, wrestling shall continue on the ground.

The wrestler who is underneath may counter the efforts of his opponent and get up.

Should one of the wrestlers go off the mat in this position, the bout shall be resumed in the centre of the mat and he shall be placed in the on-the-ground position.

When the bout is resumed, the competitor who is to adopt the on-the-ground position shall compulsorily get down on to his hands and knees on the mat, with his hands and elbows spread out and at a distance of at least 8 inches from his knees. His arms shall be stretched out and his feet not crossed. After checking the positions of both wrestlers, the referee shall blow his whistle.

The wrestler who is on top may voluntarily take up an attacking position; but he should come into contact with his opponent by placing his two hands flat on the back of the wrestler underneath, parallel to one another; the wrestler who is underneath shall be free to change the initial position only after his opponent has made the first contact by touching him on the back with both hands; he may then attack the wrestler who is on top.

The wrestler who is underneath may counter the efforts of his opponent and get up.

Should one wrestler bring his opponent down to the ground, he must be active; if both of the competitors are passive, the referee may order them to get up and to continue the bout in the standing position.

Article 20 — Wrestling shall always begin on the blowing of the referee's whistle. It shall be forbidden for the wrestler who has the on-top position to resume wrestling by jumping on his opponent; should this foul be committed, the referee shall reprimand the wrestler at fault and cause the wrestler on the ground to get up.

The wrestler in the on-top position shall not be entitled to interrupt the hold or to ask for a return to the initial position on the mat.

The End of the First or Second Period, and the End of the Bout

Article 21 — The timekeeper shall indicate the end of the first period, the second period, and likewise the end of the bout, by a stroke of the gong.

The referee shall then blow his whistle immediately to indicate either the end of the first or second period or the end of the bout. Should the referee not have heard the stroke of the gong, the Mat Chairman shall intervene and cause the bout to be brought to end.

No action shall be valid between the sounding of the gong and the blowing of the referee's whistle.

Once the bout has finished, the referee shall take up his position in the middle of the mat, facing the officials' table; the wrestlers shall shake hands and take up their positions on either side of the referee and shall await the decision of the judges and the Adjudication Board; they may not remove their anklets or pull down the shoulder-straps of their uniform before the decision has been announced.

Foul Holds

Article 22 — The pulling of hair, flesh, ears, private parts and uniform shall be forbidden. The twisting of the fingers and toes shall be forbidden. Brawling, kicking, throttling, pushing and the applying of holds liable to endanger the life of an opponent or cause a fracture or dislocation of his limbs, shall likewise be forbidden.

Holds intended to torture one's opponent or to cause him to suffer pain so that he will be compelled to give up shall likewise be forbidden.

Stepping on an opponent's feet shall be forbidden.

The touching of an opponent's face between the eyebrows and the line of the mouth shall be forbidden. The gripping of the throat shall be forbidden.

In the case of holds applied in the standing position and from behind, when the opponent is turned with his head pointing downwards (inversed waist hold), the throw shall be made solely to the side and not downwards (head-first pike); part of the body, other than the feet, of the contestant who is applying the hold must touch the mat before the upper part of the body of the contestant who is being attacked does so.

A bridge must be pressed down, i.e. it shall be forbidden to lift one's opponent when he is in the bridge position and then throw him down on the mat (severe impact with the ground); it shall likewise be forbidden to cause a bridge to collapse by pushing in the direction of the head.

The double head-hold (double Nelson) shall be permitted; however, the hold must always be applied from the side, without the legs being used in any way against any part of the opponent's body.

The bending of an opponent's arm through an angle of more than 90° shall likewise be forbidden.

Head holds using both hands shall be forbidden.

When a hold is being applied, the holding of the head shall be allowed using one arm only.

It shall be forbidden to force one's elbow or knee into the opponent's abdomen or stomach.

An opponent's arm may not be forced behind his back in such a position that his forearm and arm form a closed angle and with a pressure being applied at the same time.

The use of two arms on headlocks shall be forbidden no matter how they are applied

Contestants shall be forbidden to speak to each other during the bout.

Foul Holds — Greco-Roman Wrestling

It shall be forbidden to seize one's opponent below the hips or to grip one's opponent with one's legs.

All pushing, pressure or lifting made with the legs when in contact with a part of the opponent's body shall be forbidden.

It shall, for example, be forbidden for the attacker, while wrestling is in progress on the ground, to lift his opponent by using his legs against his knee and thigh in order to secure a fall.

Foul Holds — Freestyle Wrestling

Tripping and sideways striking with the feet or legs shall not be forbidden.

Scissors grips applied with the leg to the head or body shall be forbidden.

It shall not be necessary to accompany one's opponent to the ground when applying certain holds with the foot.

The gripping of an opponent's uniform shall be forbidden and clinging to the mat shall likewise be forbidden, both in freestyle wrestling and in Greco-Roman.

Placing in Danger

Article 23 — It shall be considered that a wrestler is in a position involving a "placing in danger" when he goes beyond the vertical line by 90° with his back turned towards the mat and resists with the upper part of his body to avoid being placed in a position in which both of his shoulders are on the mat (the fall).

The wrestler may resist with his head, elbows and shoulders.

A placing in danger shall be counted when:

a) — The wrestler who is defending forms a bridge in order to avoid a "fall.

b) — The wrestler who is defending has his back towards the mat and is resting on one or both elbows or goes down on his elbows so as to prevent himself from being brought down on both shoulders.

c) — The wrestler is lying on one shoulder while being 90° beyond the vertical line with his other shoulder.

The referee shall necessarily begin to count the seconds, up to 5, for each instantaneous position so long as the "placing in danger" continues. It shall not be counted as a "placing in danger" when a wrestler goes 90° beyond the vertical line with his chest and abdomen turned towards the mat.

A "placing in danger" shall likewise be counted if, after the upper part of his body has passed through an angle of 90°, the wrestler who is being attacked is turned with his stomach or chest towards the mat in order to be brought again into a "placing in danger" position. Rolling over from one shoulder to the other with the aid of the elbows in the forming of a bridge and vice versa shall be considered as a two points action; if the position lasts for 5 seconds, this action shall count for 3 points.

After counting the 5 seconds, the referee shall raise his hand showing three fingers to indicate to the judges that the 5 seconds have elapsed and that this action counts for 3 points.

d) The wrestler is in the position of instantaneous fall when he goes onto the two shoulders without being held there.

Cautions

Article 24 — The referee may give a caution to a wrestler who is at fault with the agreement of the two judges or following a majority vote taking into account the opinions of the members of the Adjudication Board at the time of the vote.

A caution shall be given in the following cases:

  a — Passive obstruction.
  b — Foul holds.
  c — Lack of discipline during the bout.
  d — Infringements of the rules.

A caution for passive obstruction shall be given in the cases provided for in the section of these rules entitled "Passive Obstruction."

A caution for passive obstruction may be given in any part and at any time during the bout, whether the wrestling is taking place in the standing position or on the ground; it shall be pointed out to the wrestler in question thirty seconds before the giving of the first caution that a caution will be given to him. The agreement of the judges is not needed for the making of this observation; the referee shall be entitled to make it on his own initiative.

For cases b, c and d, no such prior observation shall be made to the wrestler at fault, but the caution shall be given immediately.

The caution is pronounced publicly, the referee lifts his arm on the side of the penalized wrestler. If both wrestlers receive a warning, the referee lifts both his arms simultaneously, thus indicating that both the wrestlers have been penalized.

The giving of a caution shall be recorded on the forms of the judges and members of the Adjudication Board, even if one of the number is not in agreement.

"Automatic caution:" Should there be no action and no points scored during the first period, and no caution be given, both wrestlers shall obligatory be cautioned, even in the event of no warning preceding this "automatic caution"

Article 25 — Should, as the result of a foul hold, the competitor who has applied this hold find himself in an unfavorable position, the bout shall be continued without interruption.

Any advantages resulting from a hold which is contrary to the rules shall be cancelled, even if the contestant has already released the hold.

The irregularity shall be brought to an end by the referee without the hold being released.

In cases which involve no danger, the referee shall allow the hold to be developed and wait to see what result it brings, after which he shall be free to take action, i.e. to recognize or cancel the hold and to give a caution to the wrestler at fault.

The duties of the referee with respect to a contestant who commits an irregularity shall be as follows:

    a) — To bring an end to the irregularity.

    b) — To cause the hold to be released if it is dangerous.

    c) — To ask for a caution.

    d) — The contestant at fault may be declared the loser.

Cautions shall be given in the language of the contestant in question, if necessary through an interpreter.

It is very important, especially during periods when no action is taking place, to observe and take careful note of which of the opponents is engaging in open wrestling and which is trying to evade the combat; this is of the highest importance in the final stages of a bout; the referee should oblige the opponents to engage in real combat, by giving cautions if nothing has taken place up to that time or if the two wrestlers are showing signs of passive obstruction.

Cautions given for foul holds shall be counted together with other faults committed during the bout. A distinction must be made between the expressions "declared the loser" and "disqualified."

After 3 cautions, irrespective of the reasons for which they are given, the contestant at fault shall be declared the loser.

In the event of a caution being given, the bout shall be interrupted and likewise the timing device; the caution shall be given clearly so that the contestant and the public may fully understand why it has been given.

A caution shall however only be valid provided it is confirmed by at least 3 votes (see table) or by the majority of the votes. The judges shall underline the caution in the working column of the opponent by ringing round the figure for the point marked.

In the case of a caution for passive obstruction, the referee shall ask the judges for their opinion before interrupting the bout.

In the case of a caution for forbidden holds which involve danger, the referee shall intervene immediately and then afterwards ask for the judges' opinion before giving the caution.

Should a wrestler prevent a hold in an irregular manner — for example, in Greco-Roman, if a wrestler who has been lifted, hooks the legs of his attacker — the referee shall not blow his whistle; he shall allow the hold to be carried through if no danger of injury is involved and shall draw the attention of the judges to this infringement while it is still being made; the judges shall award points according to the merits of the case and then, immediately afterwards, a caution shall be given to the wrestler at fault.

If after a foul the attacked wrestler has fallen, this fall is not valid, and a warning must be given to the one who has committed the foul.

If the judges agree to give a warning at the end of a period and the referee has not had time to give this warning because of the gong, the warning remains valid and will be pronounced by the referee after the gong.

Should a wrestler refuse to submit to the referee's decision, the latter shall make it known to him twice in succession; should the wrestler not carry out the order after these two observations, he shall be given a caution.

In the case of a very serious irregularity, disqualification shall be pronounced immediately, by a majority vote, for the whole of the competition, with the approval of the Mat Chairman.

Passive Obstruction

Article 26 — To be considered as Passivity,
— Continual obstruction of the holds of the active contestant;
— Wilful running off the mat,

a) When a wrestler voluntarily leaves the mat, the referee shall call for "time out" and warn the wrestler at fault. Any action or lack of action to avoid wrestling and voluntarily leaving the mat shall be considered as stalling (passivity). A caution for stalling may also be given to the wrestler who pushes his opponent off the mat.

b) Should the contestant go off the mat again, either in standing position or on the ground, he shall be cautioned. However, the referee must make sure that the wrestler voluntarily went off the mat and that he was not pushed by his opponent.

c) A second caution shall be given when a contestant goes off the mat or avoids wrestling for the third time.

d) Should the contestant go off the mat or avoid wrestling again, he shall be disqualified. To disqualify a wrestler there must be a unanimous vote of the referee, the judge and the two members of the Adjudication Board.

Cautions for passivity shall be given in the following manner:

a) A first caution must always be preceded by a warning to the wrestler at fault, excepting in the event of an "automatic caution", art. 24 of the present regulations.

b) Before giving a caution, the referee shall consult the judge. In the event of a disagreement, he shall consult the members of the Adjudication Board.

— Continual lying down flat on the stomach,
and the fact of holding both of the opponent's hands with a view to preventing him from engaging the combat shall be considered as passive obstruction.

Article 27 — No special points shall be awarded for activity and activity shall not be a factor in the decision as to whether the bout has ended in a win.

Article 28 — In the case of a moving off the mat, the contestant at fault shall be given a caution, **but the referee must make certain that the contestant was not pushed off by his opponent;** in addition, the referee shall explain to the wrestler at fault the reason for this caution.

Interruption of the Bout

Article 29 — Should a contestant be obliged to interrupt the bout as a result of nose bleeding, a fall on the head or any other acceptable reason beyond his own control, the referee shall suspend the wrestling for a maximum of 5 minutes in one and the same bout.

This stoppage may be allowed in one or more periods up to a total time of 5 minutes for each wrestler; if these 5 minutes are exceeded for one and the same wrestler, the bout may not be continued; however, the injured wrestler shall be notified of the end of the period of tolerance.

Should a serious mistake be made by the judges or the referee, the Mat Chairman shall intervene and shall stop the bout by sounding the gong; after consulting the referee and the judge, he shall give a ruling with regard to the difference.

Scoring

Article 30 — The judges shall mark the wrestler's points on their scoring forms as follows:

1 point: — To a wrestler who brings down his opponent and holds him on the ground by getting on top.

— to a wrestler who reverses his opponent and holds him down.

— to a wrestler who applies a correct hold and does not cause his opponent to touch the mat with either his shoulder or head during the execution of the hold.

— a caution shall count as one point to the opponent.

2 points: — To a wrestler who applies a correct hold and places his opponent momentarily in danger (less than 5 seconds).

— to a wrestler whose opponent is in a position on both elbows and his back toward the mat less than 5 seconds, considered danger.

— to the opponent of a wrestler who touches the mat with both shoulders, will receive two points, if the wrestler in danger is not held by him during the time counted by the referee.

— to a wrestler whose opponent is in an instantaneous fall, accidental fall, or rolling fall.

3 points: — To a wrestler who keeps his opponent in danger (the shoulders forming an angle of less than 90° with the mat) for 5 seconds.

A series of rolling falls and bridges for 5 seconds, continuously, will count for 3 points.

In this case, the referee shall count the seconds.

The judges shall mark down the points as and when they are awarded in each period.

When the difference between the two opponents is less than 1 point, the bout shall be declared a draw.

Should no points have been marked down on the forms, or should the number of points awarded to both wrestlers be equal, the judges shall draw a line across both sides of their forms and shall declare the bout to have been drawn.

Should there be a difference of one or more points, the winner shall be the contestant who has the larger number of points.

To ensure a uniform marking, the actions which have resulted in the fall shall not be marked down on the scoring forms, but only the earlier actions. The mere marking down of the word "fall" shall indicate final action.

The Fall

Article 31 — Defeat by reason of a fall shall be pronounced if there is a 3-vote decision in accordance with the table given in the appendix to these Regulations.

A fall occurs when both shoulders of one contestant touch the mat simultaneously and are held there by the opponent for the period required for the referee to declare a 1-count. The referee shall strike the mat with his hand once.

For a fall on the edge of the mat to be recognized as valid, it shall be sufficient for the contestant's head and both shoulders to touch the mat at the moment of the fall.

A fall shall be valid provided the judges make no observations. Should there be a conflict of opinions when the referee consults the judges, a decision shall be arrived at in accordance with the table given in the appendix to these Regulations.

A Win on Points

Article 32 — Should there be no fall within the 9 minutes laid down for the duration of the bouts in both styles, the judges shall hand in their scoring forms to the official representative in person and he shall name the winner or decide that the bout has been drawn by basing himself on the unanimous opinion of the judges or on the majority opinion (see appendix to the Regulations).

Decisions

Article 33 — The Mat Chairman shall examine the judges' forms; should the three judges be unanimous, their decision shall be given without the forms of the Adjudication Board being consulted.

Article 34 — In international competitions, should the three judges not be unanimous, the decision shall be given by the majority of the forms the three judges and the three members of the Adjudication Board.

If there are three whites and three of the same colour, the wrestler wearing the colour mentioned shall be declared the winner.

If there are three reds and three greens, the bout shall be declared a draw.

If there are three reds and three greens, the bout shall be declared a draw.

Once the decision and the technical result have been established, no protest shall be admitted (see table in appendix).

Penalty Points

Article 35 — The results of the bouts shall be determined in the following manner, on the basis of the penalty points awarded:

A contestant who throws his opponent shall receive 0 penalty points and the loser 4 points.

If the bout ends without a fall, the Mat Chairman shall name the winner on points by basing himself on the scoring forms.

A wrestler who is declared the winner on points shall receive one penalty point and his opponent 3 points.

If the bout is declared a draw, each wrestler shall receive two penalty points.

In the event of a draw bout with no score or with one or two penalty points given for stalling, each contestant shall receive 2.5 penalty points.

In the event of a win by "evident superiority" with a difference of 10 or more than 10 points between the contestants, the result of the bout shall be: 0.5 penalty point for the winner and 3.5 penalty points for the loser

If a wrestler is disqualified, he shall receive 4 bad points.

The reason for the disqualification of a wrestler shall be marked on the scoring forms and likewise on the list.

If a wrestler injures himself independently of his opponent, he shall lose the bout and shall receive 4 penalty points while his opponent shall receive 0 points.

If a wrestler is given 3 cautions, he shall be declared the loser and shall be awarded 4 penalty points, while his opponent shall receive 0 points.

If a wrestler is injured and is obliged by the Medical Board to

143

abandon, he may be classified according to his position at the end of the competition.

After accumulating 6 bad points, a contestant shall be eliminated. Contestants eliminated in the same round shall be considered as having been eliminated at the same time.

Rules for the Final (Round Robin)

Article 36 — Competitions shall continue until no more than three remain; who shall compete in the Round Robin.

a) Wrestlers will qualify for the Round Robin with less than 6 penalty points.

b) Wrestlers with 6 or more than 6 penalty points will not be qualified for the Round Robin, excepting in the cases laid down by Article 37 of the present rules.

c) The 3 or 2 wrestlers with less than 6 penalty points shall enter in the Round Robin losing all the previously received penalty points. They shall wrestle each other for the final classification.

d) Should the Round Robin contestants have met in an earlier round, they do not meet again. The result of the bouts between them shall be considered for the final classification.

Article 37 — a) If only one contestant qualifies for the Round Robin with less than 6 penalty points, he shall be the winner. Second and third places shall be determined according to Article 38.

b) If only two contestants qualify for the Round Robin, with less than 6 penalty points, and a third contestant has received 6 penalty points in the preceding round, he will be rated third and the two wrestlers who have qualified for the Round Robin shall wrestle for 1st and 2nd places

Article 38 — Should all the Round Robin contestants have been eliminated with 6 or more than 6 penalty points in the same round, they shall be rated in the following manner:

a) The wrestler with less penalty points shall be the winner;

b) Should 2, 3 or 4 contestants have the same number of penalty points, they shall wrestle a final round to break the tie;

c) Should the contestants of this final round have met each other, the penalty points received in the bouts between them shall rate them.

Article 39 — The final classification shall be determined in the following manner:

a) The wrestler with the least number of penalty points in the Round Robin shall be the winner.

b) Should two of the three contestants in the Round Robin have an equal number of penalty points, and should one of them have defeated the other, this result shall rate them.

c) Should all wrestlers in the Round Robin have an equal number of penalty points, and should they have all met each other, the total number of penalty points received during the competition must be considered to break the tie and shall rate them.

d) Should a tie still remain, the following procedure shall rate them:

— the wrestler who has secured a greater number of falls;

— the wrestler who has scored a greater number of wins on points;

— the wrestler who has scored the least number of draw bouts;

— the wrestler who has received the least number of cautions in the Round Robin.

e) If in spite of this a tie still remains, the wrestlers shall be rated as being of equal merit.

The interpretations of these rules shall be given by the Technical Committee of the I.A.W.F.

In the event of a disagreement, the French text alone shall be considered authentic.

INTERPRETATION OF THE INTERNATIONAL WRESTLING RULES

The International Wrestling Rules include all the main paragraphs concerning the actual wrestling and the functioning of the services connected with the organization of international competitions which ensure the validity of these competitions.

The Appendix to these rules is that dynamic part of our legislation for the sport of wrestling which indiscriminately expresses our desire to see this sport develop and improve all the time and make constant progress; it gives, in the form of instructions, interpretations which are based on living examples drawn from our own experience.

This Appendix will be enlarged by standing interpretations until new paragraphs can be drawn up for inclusion in our rules.

The Technical Committee of the I.A.W.F. gives the following interpretations of certain articles of the rules, cases and examples, in the light of the experience that has been acquired.

The Calling of the Wrestlers and the Elimination of Contestants from Competitions

In the first round, and solely for the first bout in a competition for each category, a wrestler who is called to the mat shall be obliged to put in an appearance within the 5 minutes following the call. Otherwise, he shall be declared the loser and may take no further part in the competition.

For the 2nd round of the same competition, competitors shall be called 3 times, with certain short pauses of 30 seconds, in French, English and the language of the organizing country. Should a wrestler, after being thus called, fail to put in an appearance, he shall be declared the loser and shall be excluded from the subsequent bouts.

The Stopping of the Bout in the Event of a Contestant Being Injured

In the event of an injury, the waiting time may not exceed a total of 5 minutes in one and the same bout. The minutes shall be announced over the loudspeaker system. Should it be impossible for the bout to be continued after the 5 minutes have elapsed, a decision shall be given in conformity with the Regulations by the Official Doctor or the Medical Board. The wrestler may continue the competition in the following round. However, the doctor of the same nationality as the competitor may take the responsibility of having the wrestler continue.

The Appreciation of the Importance of a Hold

Should a wrestler, when applying a hold which is valid in accordance with the regulations, be held underneath by his opponent, either on all fours or flat on his stomach, a point for "bringing down to the ground" shall be awarded to the wrestler who is on top; the wrestler underneath shall receive 1 point for his previous action.

If, in a similar case, a wrestler who is attempting to apply a hold is held in a position in which he is "placed in danger," his opponent shall receive 2 or 3 points (5 seconds' rule).

In those cases in which the actions of the two wrestlers change alternately from one position to another, points shall be awarded for all the actions according to their value.

The Fall

A "fall" shall be counted when both of the wrestler's shoulders touch the mat at the same time for a 1 count.

The Gong and the Importance of the Hold

At the end of the first or second 3 minute period, a hold which has been applied between the sounding of the gong and the blowing of the referee's whistle shall not be valid since it has been applied after the sounding of the gong.

At the end of the first or second 3 minute period, and after the sounding of the gong, a hold may be valid provided it had already been started before the gong was sounded and provided it places the wrestler underneath in a position in which he is in danger of being thrown, i.e. shoulders perpendicular to the mat, with an angle of less than 90°.

A counter-attack made by the wrestler underneath after the end of a 3 minute period shall in no case be counted.

In the disputable case of a fall which occurs at the very moment at which the bout ends, the sounding of the gong shall alone be taken into account (and not the blowing of the referee's whistle).

AAU SUPPLEMENT TO THE INTERNATIONAL RULES

From time to time the AAU Wrestling Committee has recommended certain modifications in the International Regulations.

The modifications do not in any way change the mechanics of wrestling, but simply make the International Regulations more flexible to comply with certain recognized American procedure of long precedent.

1. Any American Institution or Foreign Nation may enter a maximum of three entries in a weight if they are properly certified and registered as outlined in the AAU General Rules.

2. When an organization enters more than one contestant in a weight, and in the drawing he is paired with another contestant from the same organization, his name may be redrawn so that a wrestler will not wrestle his teammate in the first round, if this is possible.

3. TEAM CHAMPIONSHIPS

   In tournaments, Team Championships shall be determined by point scores earned by individual members.

   Points shall be awarded as follows:

First Place	10 Points
Second Place	7 Points
Third Place	4 Points
Fourth Place	2 Points

   No points shall be awarded for falls in selecting a Team Championship.

4. Headgear and tights are permissible in all AAU Competition.

5. The Plastic Mat, one inch in thickness and diameters of 20 feet to 26 feet-6 inches, either square or circular in form is recommended.

6. A contestant entered in a weight class and cannot make weight for that class may enter the weight class next highest, providing he weighs in for that class.

7. Officials for Senior and Open National Championships shall consist of one Referee and three Judges for each contest.

   In Local Championships if it is not possible to supply four Officials for each mat, three may be used and the Referee will also act as a Judge.

8. In Dual Meets. An Institution or Club shall be represented by only one contestant in each weight class.

9. PROTEST TO THE JURY OF APPEAL

   Protests against the decisions of the judges or referee in a match may be made to the Jury of Appeal only in the case of a technical error by the referee, judge or judges. An example would be an error by a judge in inadvertently awarding three points to "Red" on his score sheet for a near fall, when the near fall had obviously been made by "Green", and everyone agrees. Another example would be an error by the referee in calling a fall, and stopping the match, when the proper number of judges did not agree with him. Or, should a referee not break an illegal hold used by "Red", and the advantage gained by "Red" through this hold caused "Green" to lose, this would be a technical error which could be protested.

Protests may not be made in which the opinions or judgment of the judges or referee is differed with or questioned. For example, in a series of moves, in which both wrestlers may gain and lose the advantage several times, if one judge awards "Green" three points for the holds he applied and the danger in which he put "Red", while the other two judges believe that "Red" was deserving of the most points, because of the holds he applied, no protest may be made. Nor may a protest be made if a judge gave a certain credit for a certain move which the protestor feels in his opinion was too much or too little.

Protests must be made orally within 30 minutes of the end of a match. A fee of ten ($10.00) must accompany each protest and if the protest is not allowed, the fee should be forfeited to the A.A.U.

10. No contestant shall be allowed to compete in more than one weight class in any one meet.

11. MAT CHAIRMAN — The National A.A.U. and the United States Olympic Wrestling Committees have adopted the use of five officials in all A.A.U. Wrestling in the United States. The officials are: three judges, mat chairman and referee. The mat chairman will replace the three jury members as called for in the rules.

The Mat Chairman will be in charge of all other officials at the mat. He will keep a Judge's score sheet, cast his vote and make decisions in the match as the three Judges do. He may initiate the calling of falls or cautions. After a decision has been confirmed by the Mat Chairman, no protest will be recognized. If a match is not being conducted according to the rules, he may intervene immediately to straighten out the difficulty. It may be necessary to momentarily take time out.

Table I

Red	Green	White	Winner
3	1	0	Red
3	0	1	Red
2	1	1	Red
2	0	2	Red
1	3	0	Green
0	3	1	Green
1	2	1	Green
0	2	2	Green
1	0	3	Draw
0	1	3	Draw
1	1	2	Draw
2	2	0	Draw

Table for determining a fall, caution, disqualifications and other questions when five votes are cast (3 Judges, Mat Chairman and Referee).

When a majority (3 or 4) or unanimous (5) votes are cast in favor of a fall, warning or disqualification, it is a valid decision.

Table II

Referee	Judges	Mat Chairman	Results
1	3	1	Valid
1	3	0	Valid
1	2	0	Valid
0	1	1	Valid
0	3	1	Valid
0	3	0	Valid
0	2	1	Valid
1	1	0	Not Valid
1	0	1	Not Valid
0	1	1	Not Valid
0	2	0	Not Valid
1	0	0	Not Valid
0	1	0	Not Valid
0	0	1	Not Valid

INTERNATIONAL LANGUAGE AND SIGNS

The following terminology and illustrations are meant to clarify for the wrestler and official, some of the procedures governing the conduct of a bout. In many instances in international competition the referee does not speak the language of either competitor or the judges and therefore must communicate through signs. When it is necessary to converse, the official language of the F.I.L.A. is French.

Start of Bout—Wrestlers shake hands go to their respective places and await referee's whistle.

Stop—Used when contestant is running.

Passivete (Pa-se-ve-tay)—warning for stalling. Referee points at offending wrestler.

Attention—(Ah-tahn-shi-oon)—Remark before caution.

Consultation—Referee consults judges regarding cautions or other penalties.

(2)   (3)

Avertissement—Caution. Referee stops bout and holds wrist of offending wrestler, raising his other arm with clenched fist (Illustration 2.) In case of a double caution, referee holds both arms up with fists clenched (Illustration 3.)

Activity—Expression for stimulating wrestling (speed it up)

Continue—Ordering the contestants to continue wrestling.

Intervention—Judge calling referee's attention by holding flag or paddle aloft.

Chronometre—Clock—calling attention to timekeeper.

Gong—Starting bell.

Centre—Return to center of the mat. Arm signal and whistle.

Juge—Judge.

Arbitre—Referee.

Jury—Jury.

Par Terre—Mat Wrestling. Referee takes wrestlers by wrist and points to down position. (Art. 19)

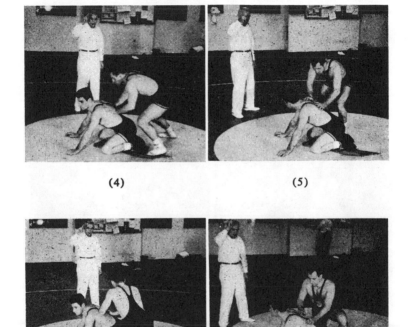

(4)   (5)

(6)   (7)

Contact—To place hands on opponent's back in starting position in Par Terre. (Art. 19). Illustrations 4, 5, 6, 7, depict legal starting positions to start or resume wrestling on the ground.

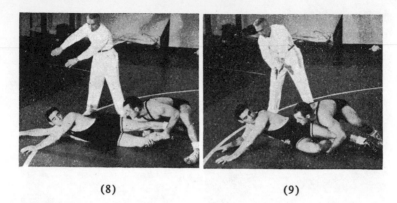

(8)   (9)

Aout—Out—Off the mat—(Illustration 8)—Takedown is not good, (Illustration 9)—Action is good, takedown is allowed.

No—Expression of disagreement.

OK—Referee uses OK signal when action near edge of mat is within bounds. Thumb and first finger closed.

(10)   (11)

Time Out—Form letter "T" with fingers of both hands (Illustration 10)

Up—Return to standing position referee, both hands pointing up. (Illustration 11)

Danger—When opponent's back is placed in exposed position to mat, and points are awarded accordingly. (Art. 30)

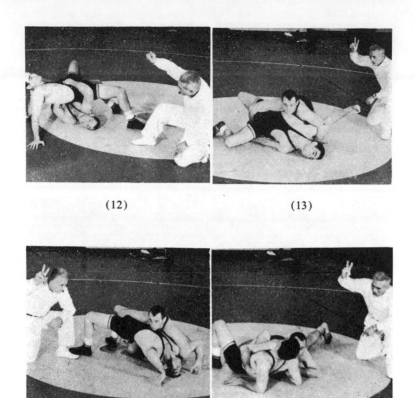

(12)   (13)

(14)   (15)

1 point—Exposing opponent's shoulders to mat, but shoulder or head does not touch mat. (Illustration 12)

2 points—Exposing opponent's shoulders to mat with head or shoulders touching mat for less than required for fall (Illustrations 13, 14); also if exposed with both elbows touching. (Illustration 15)

3 points—Holding opponent in danger for 5 seconds or more. Referee counts seconds visually. (Illustration 16).

Touche—(Toosh)—Fall—Referee has counted off full second and raises his hand to indicate fall. (Illustration 17)

(16)   (17)

(18)   (19)

Salut—End of bout when wrestlers must again shake hands.

Nul—Draw—upon sign from judges for a draw, referee raises arms of both wrestlers. (Illustration 18)

Victoire—The winner. Referee holds wrist of both wrestlers until judges signal winner. Then referee raises the arm of the victor. (Illustration 19)

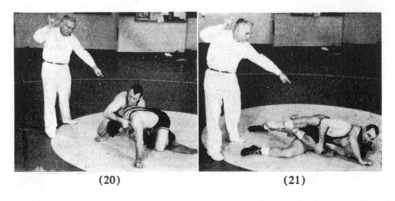

(20)   (21)

154

(22)   (23)

Three Quarter Nelson—Both hands interlocked at defender's neck —Illegal (Illustration 20).

Closed Body scissors—Illegal (Illustration 21)

Arms locked on opponent's head without an arm—Illegal (Illustrations 22 and 23)

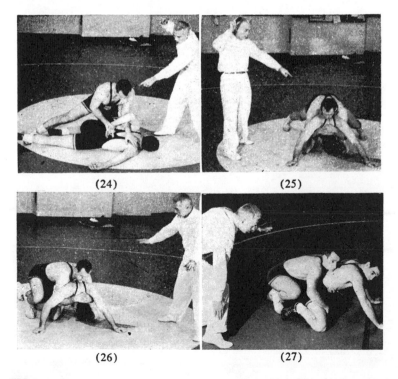

(24)   (25)

(26)   (27)

Forcing arm behind back past right angle—Illegal (Illustration 24)
Full Nelson from behind—Illegal (Illustration 25)

Full Nelson from side with legs passive—Legal (Illustration 26)

In Greco-Roman wrestling, wrestler blocks opponent's leg with his
arm (Illegal)—referee indicates by touching his own leg and pointing to offending wrestler. (Illustration 27)

Compter—To count.

Defait—Defeat.

Protest—Protest.

Fin—End of bout.

Foul—Illegal hold.

Index